By the Same Author

Susan Lee's ABZ's of Economics

Susan Lee's ABZ's of Money and Finance

SUSAN LEE

SIMON & SCHUSTER

New York London Toronto

Sydney Tokyo Singapore

WHY THE GOVERNMENT

IS A MENACE

TO ECONOMIC HEALTH

HANDS

OFF

SIMON & SCHUSTER
Rockefeller Center
1230 Avenue of the Americas
New York, NY 10020

SIMON & SCHUSTER and colophon are registered trademarks
of Simon & Schuster Inc.

Designed by Jennifer Ann Daddio

Manufactured in the United States of America

1   3   5   7   9   10   8   6   4   2

Library of Congress Cataloging-in-Publication Data
Lee, Susan.
Hands off: why the government is a menace to economic health/Susan Lee.
p.   cm.
1. United States—Economic policy—1993–   2. United States—Economic policy—
1981–1993. 3. United States—Economic policy.
I. Title.
HC106.82.L44   1996
338.973—dc20   95-47186
ISBN 0-684-81442-0

To two totally brilliant, absolutely amusing and
completely exasperating editors,
Bob Bartley and Jim Michaels.
I know, I know; you aren't going to like everything in this book—
but without your many years of help and guidance,
it wouldn't have been written. Thank you.

CONTENTS

Introduction:
Dangerous Delusion

This is a book about the economy. It assumes that most everybody wants a strong, healthy, growing economy. And, since most everybody has opinions and ideas about how to get there, this is also a book about policy. Even economic policies that are specifically targeted to promote trade or give money to poor people or tax capital gains are all driven by the belief that they ultimately will improve the economy. That's certainly the way it's been and probably the way it will continue. Except for one thing. Economic policy—especially the way it's been done for the past 35 years—doesn't work. Indeed, the notion that policy has the power and talent to deliver a strong, healthy, growing economy is a delusion.

This is a difficult message for the simple reason that it runs contrary to how we think about economic life. And, in attacking the conventional wisdom, I am mindful of the fact that my argument should be as complete as possible. Thus, this book comes at its message from four distinct perspectives. Part I is an up-close-and-personal look at how economic policy affects our daily lives. Parts II and III take a step back to consider how the currently fashionable way of thinking about policy took hold and has produced today's economic mess. Part IV offers a better way to think about policy, and part V takes another step back to offer a decade-by-decade illustration of how this new view provides a more satisfying explanation of economic events. The sermon exhorting us to cast off our benighted attitude toward an activist government comes in the Conclusion.

We establish government in part because it makes it easier to facilitate our economic wishes and needs. Most basically, the government takes money from us and then spends it on things most of us presumably want. If we think that government should give unemployed people a helping hand, it does. If we want to give money to victims of floods or droughts or other natural disasters, it will. Government will also support a military and diplomatic establishment to keep us safe from our enemies. It will explore space and undertake other forms of big, pricey research to improve our lives. And so on and so forth. Generally speaking, the things that government does are not evil. They are undertaken with the best of intentions and the assumption that government can do certain things better than can private—individual or collective—efforts.

That's not to say that government doesn't do stupid, wasteful, or destructive things. It does—usually unintentionally and to its own great surprise. In fact, it is fair to say that the more government does, the greater the chances that it will produce stupid, wasteful, and destructive results.

But recognizing that an activist government can be counterproductive is not the same as criticizing government, complaining that the bureaucracy is too large and inefficient, or that Congress is hostage to special interests, or that whoever is president is politically inept. This class of critiques argues that if government were structured differently or had different leadership or were run more efficiently, it would function better and, in functioning better, would yield better results. This argument gives the impression of knowing cynicism or sophistication, but it is still based on a delusion.

The plain fact is that government cannot fix economic problems. Rather, government activism often results in regulatory gridlock, produces unintended consequences, and/or creates an environment of uncertainty. What government can do, to a larger or lesser degree, is to make it difficult for us to solve problems or, at best, it can create a congenial climate for us to fix things. Once we get that through our heads and our hearts, economic life will be a lot more tolerable.

When I started writing about economic policy in the mid-1970s, I focused on smaller things—regulations gone bad, laws with unintended consequences. But my bottom line was always that if government were a little smarter, or a tad more agile, it could make things right. That's what I had been taught by professors with models and equations that I dutifully and confidently copied into my notebook. Indeed, that's what I taught to my students, who dutifully and confidently copied them into their notebooks.

In the late 1970s, when I started to pay attention to what was actually going on in the real world, I began to suspect that this idea was a lot of hooey. I voted for Jimmy Carter, a smart guy with a bunch of detailed ideas about managing the economy, but the economy got worse. I did not vote for Ronald Reagan first time around, scorning him as a good-natured guy with a simple vision, but the economy got better. What was I missing? Perhaps there was something more than economic policies at work? Perhaps there were forces stronger or more intelligent than "enlightened" government? And if so, then why were we—the policy mongers—so besotted with the idea of moving government policy one way and then another? This is what I found.

- Government activism is not an idea that was foisted on an unsuspecting public by manipulative Beltway types. It is the organic result of an economic theory—Keynesianism—that had the very best academic credentials and was embraced in the 1960s, first by politicians and government bureaucrats and then by a public dispirited by U.S. economic performance in the previous decade.
- The idea actually seemed to work in practice. The Keynesians conquered Washington in the early 1960s, asking government to take an active hand in the country's economic destiny. Government did so and—*voila!*—economic growth perked up. It never occurred to most people that this was a fortuitous coincidence.
- The relationship between the practice of this theory and strong economic performance was indeed a fortuitous coincidence. Growth would have been supranormal in the 1960s in any case because of a number of encouraging global factors.
- In the 1970s, when the economy slumped and it became clear that government activism was not capable of delivering economic growth year after year, a great puzzlement set in. Academic chieftains pushed and pulled at Keynesian theory, trying to get it to come right. Politicians applied its tenets more feverishly, trying to get it to come right. Of course, nothing came right; indeed, the economy got worse, and that, too, was mostly a coincidence, due to many factors well beyond the sphere of activist policy.
- By the 1980s, there was a body of economic thought that explained why government activism could not work. But for vari-

ous reasons—the idea was so contrarian, so against the grain of what many people wanted to believe—it was mostly ignored. And, anyway, the 1980s marked a return to more normal economic growth patterns, again mostly for reasons that had little to do with activist policy.

- So far, the economy of the 1990s has been disappointing, and misguided policy bears much of the blame.

The short of what I found is that government activism—no matter how pure of purpose, how cleverly planned and executed—has three results: it gives rise to unintended consequences, it creates uncertainty and promotes short-term thinking in the private sector, and it leads to government regulation of many aspects of the economy that should be left alone. When we are lucky, only one of these results occurs; most often, however, all three are present.

Like all authors, I am going to say that my argument is particularly important today. Right now, at this minute, the United States is at an economic turning point. The chief rival to our economic system, socialism, has been discredited. Our own system, liberal capitalism (or whatever you choose to call it), is victorious but wheezing a bit. It doesn't seem to be as vigorous as it once was.

In short, many people feel that since we're not such hot stuff either, it's time to set off in a different direction. Two other roads beckon. The current administration is pushing the country down the one leading to more government activism, more government solutions. I hope to convince you that this involves a dangerous delusion about government competence and power and that the other road, the one that leads to less government and more steady policies, is the way to go.

Again, let me say that as a once-and-future policy bigmouth, it's very hard to give up the notion that a healthy economy depends on government having a comprehensive, detailed, and activist (always prepared to change) policy. Rather, a healthy economy depends on the government standing back and letting us go to work. And that advice goes double when a big bad event hits the economy and makes many of us unhappy. All of our tiny little private responses will go a longer way to making things right again than any of the things government might try.

I think my argument is a strong one. I also know that the difficulties in convincing you are not only with the message, but also with the fact that this is a book about economics. And, as an economist, I understand why lots of people don't like to read economics books. I've nodded my head up and down hundreds of times while listening to their reasons: economics is dreary and dismal, economists make economics unnecessarily hard to understand, none of it matters anyway because economists disagree with one another all the time, and economics is cold and hard-hearted. Each of these arguments contains some truth; but consider them in turn.

- Economics is dull. This is mostly true. But since economic forces determine the way the world works, mastering some economics provides two benefits—the virtue that comes with doing something unpleasant and an understanding of what is going on so that one can behave in an enlightened way.
- Economics is difficult because economists are obscurantists. Mostly true again. But it is also true that understanding economics does take more than a few minutes of thought, requires some rigor in argument, and depends on a working knowledge of several buzzwords. Yet that doesn't mean that the basic drill is difficult. Economics is a way of interpreting the effect of incentives on behavior. This everybody understands. It's also a way of explaining Adam Smith's notion of the invisible hand—when everybody is free to pursue his or her self-interest, the result benefits

the entire society—which is also quite intuitive. It's trite to say, but people do make everyday decisions on the basis of some economic model—whether it's called price theory or common sense.

- It doesn't matter because even economists can't agree. That's only a little true. Economists actually agree on more than they disagree on, and their disagreements tend to be politically generated. To be sure, as a science, economics is probably more like sociology and less like physics, but that doesn't mean its insights are any less important—especially if the political component is discounted. (For example, in my case, as a mild libertarian, you might want to discount my ranting about government regulation . . . but just slightly.)

- Economics is hard-hearted. I am not sure that has any truth, but I understand why it seems that way—economics doesn't deal comfortably with or speak softly about social issues. Often, talk about free markets is taken to mean a system of unfettered selfishness or rapacious capitalism; talk about efficiency is taken to mean a system of brutal survival of the fittest. Nonetheless, people are motivated to study economics because they want to "improve" economic circumstances, and that is a social as well as an economic goal.

This book has a few peculiarities for one dealing with economics; most notably, it doesn't have a lot of numbers. (What!! Why not?) For several reasons: It is fairly easy to find economic data on almost anything that does exist in the economy and then present it in such a way that backs up almost any argument. This is especially true when looking at small events over short periods of time. I have tried to avoid that temptation. The numbers I do use are as broadly expressed as possible. In taking, as this book does, a 35-year view, it's really the direction of events, or the trend, that

matters. It is more illuminating to know if whatever is being measured mostly goes up over time, or mostly down, or stays pretty
much constant; the only deviations that are important are those
that stand out over several periods.

Also, the statistics that do matter are, whenever possible, expressed as a share of the economy as represented by gross national product (GNP) or by gross domestic product (GDP)—the
value of all the goods and services in the economy, all the haircuts,
hamburgers, trucks, dental services, and so on; in other words, the
number that captures how much the economy is worth. The reason for this is simple; it's one of the few numbers that assess impact on the economy. For instance, a favorite trick in talking about
the budget deficit is to express it in absolute dollars because the
number is big and scary and reveals little. For example, the federal
budget deficit in 1982 was $150 billion after inflation, and in 1990,
it was almost $200 billion after inflation. Looks like the deficit got
worse, doesn't it? But, actually, even though the number in 1990 is
bigger and badder, as a share of the economy, it represents less
damage—the difference between 4.1 percent in 1982 and 4 percent
in 1990—because the value of the economy grew, too.

Another thing to keep in mind is that data change. This is especially true for figures that have a wide following. To satisfy this
audience, the main creator of data, the federal government, issues
an estimate of the number as soon as it can, then reissues another
estimate when the data are more complete, publishes that number
as fact and then changes it later when the data are still better. Even
then, when the numbers are thought to be solid, everything might
change when the benchmarks are changed. (The National Income
and Product Accounts, the mother for most data, went through a
benchmark revision in 1985 and the numbers changed.) Too,
sometimes the government will transform a whole category of
measurement. In 1991, for instance, the familiar category called

gross national product (GNP)—one that economists and everyone else had been using without complaint for decades—was transformed into a new category, gross domestic product (GDP). The latter counts only the value of goods and services within the borders of the United States.

Although I have tried to be evenhanded in my descriptions of various policies, the focus is uneven. Fiscal policy (government taxation and spending) dominates the discussion, while monetary policy (the Federal Reserve's decision to make more, or less, money available to the economy) is given minor attention. That's not because monetary policy is any less important than fiscal policy—it isn't. Rather, because the design of fiscal policy has so many more possibilities and because it is so much more fun to practice than monetary policy, it has always received more than its due.

And, finally, although this book has a political as well as an economic point, there is very little description of the Inside the Beltway he-said, she-said stuff. For my purposes, economic ideas are more important than the political process. This book is not, and doesn't intend to be, an insiders' account of the political process. To be sure, the political process changes and distorts ideas, but it turns out that by sticking to the economic arguments in their most pristine form, we get a better notion of intentions. Such an approach offers not only a glimpse of how people are thinking about problems, but it also allows their solutions the benefit of the doubt.

And that is why the focus is on the various administrations rather than on Congress: It is the president who chooses the rhetoric and substance of the economic policy debate, both as the main spokesperson for the nation and as the appointer of the Council of Economic Advisers, the secretaries of the Treasury and Commerce, the U.S. Trade Representative, and heads of other economic agencies. That is also why, of these agencies, the focus is on the Council of Economic Advisers, which is staffed by academic economists who always have one eye on not embarrassing themselves with the rest of the profession. The same professionalism does not hold for economic documents or utterances from other parts of the administration that are much more political.

As for those documents and utterances, the Council of Economic Advisers obligingly publishes every year, in late winter, a massive document known as the *Economic Report of the President.* The *Report* not only contains hundreds of pages of figures on almost everything the federal government measures, but, in addition, its two prose sections represent the economic thinking of the administration in its most scholarly form. The first section is a letter from the president and the second is written by the Council's economists.

Of course, every so often it's necessary to do a reality check on how regular people are thinking about things. For this purpose, I did not rely exclusively on the standard business and financial publications, like the *Wall Street Journal* or *Business Week* magazine, on the grounds that their audiences tend to be more sophisticated than a general audience. Instead, I have leaned on *Time* magazine's coverage of the economic scene. Having looked at other general news publications, I found that during the 1960s and 1970s, *Time* was about the only mass-circulation magazine that regularly included economics as part of its general news coverage—the editors even convened a Board of Economists over the years who met regularly in *Time*'s offices to talk about the economy. Not only did many, many people read *Time*, it was taken seriously and took itself seriously as the interpreter of events for the literate middle class. It both shaped and reflected public opinion.

In the end, this book is about ideas—how the economy works, what the proper role of government is, and how to get the most out of the intersection of the two. It's easy to blame an economic mess on politics, particularly on what happens to ideas once they get to Congress, but bad ideas are worse than bad politics. It's the ideas we have to get straight first.

We are in a position to roar into the millennium (if you'll pardon the phrase). The last half of the 1990s could make a stellar decade. Many of the factors that stimulate economic growth are in place. What remains is for the lessons of the 1960s about what actually propels economic growth, the lessons of the 1970s about the mischief of an overactive government, and the lessons of the 1980s about the virtues of less government to be absorbed.

The giant sweep by the Republican party in the 1994 congressional elections, which was a big surprise to most professional political types, including, I suspect, to many Republicans, demonstrated that the voters were ready to reverse the direction of ever more government. The most consistent polling result showed that voters felt that government had become too big, too expensive, and too intrusive. But beyond that message was the fact that voters were fed up, period. And that is not a frivolous sentiment, either. The next section, which presents an intimate look at the impact of government activism, shows why that is the case.

Part I

How Big, Busy Government Affects Daily Life

Uncertainty: The Stock Market Crash of 1987

O n Friday, October 16, 1987, the Dow Jones Industrial Average plunged 108 points. It was a record drop. I remember it with painful clarity, not because I lost a ton of money, but because that evening I appeared on ABC-TV's "Nightline" to talk about it. I was supposed to discuss what the plunge meant to the economy, but because ABC had live and dramatic footage of little Jessica McClure being pulled out of a well in Texas, the discussion was reduced to a few minutes. No time for blather with plenty of on-the-one-hand-on-the-other. Instead, Ted Koppel asked me what would happen when the market opened for trading on Monday. Probably go up, I said.

Hah.

On Monday, October 19, when I got to my office at *Forbes* magazine at 9:30, I turned on my Quotron. I watched the symbol for the Dow Jones Industrial Average blink: down 67 points on opening, blink . . . down 82, blink . . . down 97, blink . . . down 106. By late that morning, many stocks were closed for trading. Their symbols appeared on the screen followed by dots where the price quotations usually ran. I had never seen anything like it.

By the end of trading on Black Monday, the Dow Jones had lost 23 percent of its value; the Standard & Poor's Index of 500 stocks was down 29 percent. It was the greatest collapse of wealth in history—some $1 trillion had vanished.

At the time, lots of people thought Black Monday was going to be just like 1929, when the stock market crashed consequent to the Great Depression. It wasn't. It wasn't even close. Indeed, it proved to be a financial oddity.

Nonetheless, the market crash of 1987 makes an interesting illustration of how government micromanagement of the economy can draw an unproductive response from people, generate a lot of second guessing, and unsettle the economy. Interestingly, it was caused in very large part by the sudden reversal of the Reagan administration's commitment to let the economy struggle through tough spots on its own, notably its refusal to "manage" the value of the dollar on the foreign exchange markets. That reversal created mega-uncertainty for investors and they responded by fleeing the equity markets.

Even though Black Monday had followed a very bad Friday for the market, chances are that nothing much would have happened on Monday had it not been for the administration's mucking up an already bad situation over the weekend. This is not to say that top policy makers were solely responsible for the debacle. Rather, these policy makers dropped the match on a volatile mix that had been building for several months. Consider:

Beginning in the summer of 1987, and accelerating into the fall, there was a marked change in investors' confidence as the conditions that had promoted a long economic expansion started to sour. The bull market had begun in 1982 as the economy was pulling out of a nasty recession. Inflation and interest rates were low, and tax changes in 1981 promised plump corporate earnings. Conditions were perfect for a strong stock market and, unsurprisingly, investors started buying stocks.

Nonetheless, for the next five years, the stock market adhered to the Wall Street adage that bull markets climb a wall of worry. Despite the fact that the economy tooled along, growing at a respectable annual rate and that unemployment marched steadily down, the professional worriers were busy. They fretted over the ballooning trade and budget deficits. These deficits, said the worriers, could not continue without bad effect. Eventually, they warned, interest rates would rise, choking off the business expansion and tipping the economy into a recession. Too, the worriers were concerned about the dollar—it was too strong, they tut-tutted, and exporters would suffer.

For the most part, the Reagan administration had paid little attention to the worriers. For five years, it held to its position that the value of the dollar should be determined by the foreign exchange markets—that the dollar should be allowed to float, finding its own level against other currencies. In 1985, however, the Reagan team gave in to the professional worriers and began to tinker. This policy shift proved to be the first tiny step toward a large mistake.

In early fall of 1985, the Group of Seven industrial nations agreed, in the Plaza accord, that the dollar was too strong and should be brought down. Their reasoning was that a weaker dollar would make imports more expensive, thus reducing domestic demand for them; at the same time, a weaker dollar would make exports cheaper, thus increasing foreign demand. The hope, in other words, was that a weaker dollar would lead to a smaller trade deficit.

During the two years following the Plaza accord, the Federal

Reserve busily intervened in the foreign exchange markets to lower the value of the dollar. And the dollar fell 30 to 40 percent against the currencies of our major trading partners. Nonetheless, the trade deficit did not improve. Moreover, both interest rates and inflation started to head up. Now the worriers really did have something to gnaw over.

By late summer 1987, the wall of worry had become too steep for the stock market to climb. On August 25, the Dow Jones Industrial Average peaked at 2722, up 40 percent for the year. It then started to drift down as investors, spooked by rising rates and the growing possibility that a recession was in the cards, started to sell stocks. By mid-October, the Dow Jones had lost over 200 points. Investors were wary and jumpy. Professional forecasters were tripping over one another in their rush to predict the start of a recession. And Wall Street's stock jockeys, always a superstitious bunch, thought they had received a sign that the end was near—the cover story of *Fortune* magazine featured Alan Greenspan, the chairman of the Federal Reserve, making bullish remarks.

No question that the atmosphere on Wall Street was hair-trigger: One little real event could have caused a sell-off. But instead of one little event, the stock market was hit by several medium-size pieces of bad news and a major policy blunder by the Reagan administration.

First, the economic data seemed to confirm fears that the economy was slipping into a recession. On Wednesday, October 14, the government announced that the merchandise trade deficit for August was well over a billion dollars more than anticipated. Foreign exchange traders rushed to sell the dollar, which then fell smartly against the deutsche mark and the yen. In the bond market, traders immediately off-loaded 30-year Treasury bonds, causing interest rates to inch over the 10 percent mark for the first time in two years. Both the fall in the dollar and the rise in interest rates drove the stock market down.

The market was further shaken by the announcement that the House Ways and Means Committee had produced legislation to eliminate certain tax benefits used to finance corporate takeovers. This was a particularly alarming bit of news: Stocks of companies involved in takeovers—called deal stocks—had been an engine of the bull market. Risk arbs (the slang for professional money managers who buy big chunks of deal stocks, betting their value will rise when a takeover is announced) rushed to sell their deal stocks. In the quaintly apt phase, there were more sellers than buyers, and the market closed down 95 points.

On Thursday, more bad news. Retail sales figures for September were announced; they were down from the previous month, mostly due to lagging auto sales. Chemical Bank raised its prime lending rate by half a percentage point to 9.75, the highest in two years. The dollar fell again against the yen and the deutsche mark. The Dow Jones ended the day down another 57 points. By Friday, investors were itchy. Many were holding stocks that had risen smartly since the start of the bull market. Should they sell and take their gains before the recession took hold? Should they sit tight and wait for the spate of bad news to pass?

Peggy Forbes, a broker in Merrill Lynch's Fifth Avenue office in New York City, went to work at 6:00 A.M. Friday morning. She knew many of her clients were poised to get out of the market. She had already put in long hours on the phone on Wednesday and Thursday discussing alternative investments with nervous investors. By Friday's market opening, she was ready with various game plans—bonds, real estate, and money market funds. "I knew Friday was going to be a zoo," she said. "I canceled my Friday-evening flight to Boston to visit my kids. I was ready for the deluge."

She was prescient. Many of her clients—indeed, many investors—decided to cash in. The market was swamped by waves of selling. It ended the day with two new records: the largest single-day drop in history—the Dow Jones was down 108 points—and the heaviest single-day volume—344 million shares traded. Peggy Forbes never got to Boston; she spent the weekend in New York catching up on Friday's paperwork.

Investors had a lot to contemplate over the weekend. The bump-up in interest rates was the worst news. During the five-year run of the bull market, it had become fashionable to say that stocks were driven by interest rates. When interest rates rose, investors sold stocks because higher rates increased the likelihood of an economic slowdown and decreased the desirability of holding lower-yielding stocks. The fact that interest rates had just pierced the psychologically important barrier of 10 percent was sobering.

So, too, the fall in the value of the dollar was troublesome. In February 1987, the Group of Seven, meeting in Paris, had decided that the dollar had fallen enough; they declared a new policy to hold the dollar steady. Declaration, however, is a lot easier than achievement. And every time the dollar slipped in value, there was a lot of scary talk about the dollar being "out of control" or in a "free fall." If the dollar plunged, foreign investors would liquidate their dollar-denominated assets lickety-split, thereby causing a collapse in stock prices.

And, finally, investors had to contend with that slippery notion called investor psychology. If the market looks like it's heading down, investors will want to dump their stocks; if the market looks like it's heading up, investors will want to buy. This bit of fatuous thinking even has the status of a saying on Wall Street: "The trend is your friend." Fatuous it may be, but few investors have the courage to buck a trend. And the trend in October certainly seemed to be down.

Simply put, any investor worth his or her brokerage commissions was contemplating his or her strategy over that October weekend, and the contemplation had to have been a rather gloomy exercise.

With a startling display of insensitivity toward the shaky condition of the financial markets, Secretary of the Treasury James Baker picked this moment to bad-mouth the dollar. Baker was angry with the Germans, who had been bumping up their interest rates since August and had just bumped them up again. Higher German rates, of course, make their bond market more attractive to investors and bid money away from the U.S. market; higher rates were also slowing the German economy, making it less likely to buy U.S. exports.

On Saturday, Baker remarked that Germany "should not expect us to sit back here and accept" increases in their interest rates. On Sunday, however, the *New York Times* carried a page-one story reporting that a senior administration official—widely believed to be Baker—had said that the United States would allow the dollar to fall against the deutsche mark. Not only was this an abrupt departure from U.S. policy to hold the dollar steady, it also seemed to be the opening gun in a devaluation race. Suddenly, a "free fall" scenario didn't seem far-fetched. Suddenly, dollar-denominated assets—and the U.S. economic environment itself—seemed less hospitable and fraught with uncertainty.

No doubt Baker felt that his public temper tantrum was justified. But there is also no doubt that Baker failed miserably to take into account the impact his statements would have on the market. He thought that threatening the Germans would strengthen the dollar, and hence the stock market. But his tantrum panicked investors. Moreover, the globalization of the financial markets makes it possible for investors all over the world to react speedily to economic conditions in the United States. And when the secretary of the treasury implies a policy shift that promises to hammer the dollar into the ground, investors react.

When Monday morning dawned in the world's markets, investors were clamoring to sell. Twelve hours before Wall Street knew what hit it, the Asian markets opened and prices plunged. Tokyo, Hong Kong, and Singapore opened down. So did Australia, followed by the European markets—Frankfurt, Amsterdam, London, and Brussels dove. By the time the New York Stock Exchange opened, the backlog of sell orders was enough to drop the index almost 70 points at the bell.

By the end of the day, observers and players alike had been awed by the drama, sickened by the fact, and made dizzy by the speed. Doubtless, the crash was a stunning event by itself. But it was also a stunning demonstration of the power of government to create mischief—to generate unproductive second-guessing in the private sector in response to uncertainty and to cause unintended consequences.

Granted, part of the crash was due to a worsening of the economic fundamentals that had underwritten a five-year business expansion like rising interest and inflation rates. But the crash was surely triggered by wrong-thinking government policy. Baker thought his threats against the German central bank would stabilize interest rates and reassure the financial markets. That piece of hubris was severely punished. He created instead a sharp crack of pessimism, panicked investors into a selling stampede, and caused chaos in the very markets he hoped to calm.

But, remarkably, the administration realized its mistake, and its subsequent actions did much to avert long-term damage to the economy. Immediately after the crash, cries went up for the government to do something. The professional worriers came out in force. Some drew parallels with the stock market crash of 1929 and warned that a full-scale depression loomed. There were loud voices calling for an immediate reduction in the federal budget deficit (the standard culprit when anything went wrong), and there were also demands to reregulate the financial industry and regulate the financial markets.

The latter demand was more than just sour grapes. Starting in the late 1960s, the financial industry had undergone a period of deregulation. The move to free the markets from government control was spurred by many events: a general push to deregulate huge sectors of the economy, like telecommunications and transportation; globalization of the world's markets, made possible by advances in technology; economic conditions, like high inflation and interest rates and floating exchange rates; and a burst of innovation in financial instruments.

One by one, the monopolies created by the New Deal were exposed to the chilly breath of competition. In 1970, the Federal Reserve removed ceilings on interest rates for bank deposits of more than $100,000 with maturities of less than six months, thereby freeing banks to compete with one another for funds. Five years later, the Securities and Exchange Commission ordered brokers to stop fixing commissions on stock sales, thus promoting competition in the brokerage industry. In 1977, Merrill Lynch introduced its cash management account, enabling it to compete with banks for funds. In 1980 and 1982, the Federal Reserve allowed banks to pay interest on checking accounts and removed all ceilings on interest rates, permitting banks to fight back against the brokerage houses.

The history of the deregulation of the financial industry is complicated. But the net has been just what any economics text predicts: An increase in competition led to lower prices and more choices for consumers and encouraged innovation and productivity. Needless to say, deregulation also created losers. Without the shelter of a monopoly lock on markets, uncompetitive businesses suffered; many failed. These failures generated a constituency for reregulation of the industry.

Regulation was also the plat du jour for two other groups. The long climb of the bull market encouraged many investors to forget the fact that the stock market carries risk. They felt entitled to riskless returns on their investments. Investors who thought the market was perfect when it went up, felt betrayed when it went down and demanded that the government "insure" them against losses. Too, there was the permanent constituency who feel that the government's role is to make right what has gone wrong.

After Black Monday, these voices became loud and passionate. Still, nothing much came of the cries for the government to do something. Rather, five factors ensured a do-nothing response.

The first—and by no means as slight as it sounds—was President Reagan's reflexive hands-off policy. Reagan endured a lot of criticism for his indifference to the crash, but it was this indifference that set the tone for what followed. His initial response was casual. Beneath the whoosh of his helicopter's blades, on the night of Friday, October 16, after a record market loss, Reagan shouted some platitudes to reporters. And, on Black Monday, he sought to reassure, saying that the economy was sound and the market had just been hit by "profit-taking."

The press was livid. Editorial writers at the *Washington Post* and the *New York Times* frothed and foamed. Business publications were stuffed with articles excoriating him for his lack of understanding of the economy and the markets; the *Wall Street Journal* ran story after story of small investors who had been devastated. The national newsmagazines were outraged. *Time* magazine, for example, ran a November cover story headlined "Who's in Charge: The Nation Calls for Leadership, and There Is No One Home." Despite the hysteria, the Reagan administration did the minimum. It convened a commission to look into the reasons for the crash.

A second reason for government restraint was a generalized version of the first reason: The country had already experienced almost eight years of an administration whose primary ideological message was "We can't help" and whose major economic response was "We can't afford it." Neither of these views had brought rack and ruin. To the contrary, the last five years had been good. Economic growth had been surprisingly strong and unemployment surprisingly low. It was almost as if the country had gotten sufficiently up the learning curve on both these ideological and economic views to temper anxiety over a minimalist government.

Third, it wasn't clear just how serious the economic crisis was. The disappearance of $1 trillion in wealth seems like a serious event. But it was, after all, paper wealth. The assets that the paper represented were still in place. Simply put, it was not as if a bomb had exploded, destroying factories, machines, labor, managerial talent, fax machines, or cars in parking lots. The assets remained—they were just worth less.

There were, in fact, compelling reasons to devalue those assets. Aside from the broad expectation that a recession loomed, a somewhat more narrow look puts the change in values in perspective. Before the crash, price/earnings ratios averaged around 22. (A price/earnings ratio is the market value of one share of stock over its earnings per share. Generally speaking, the higher the ratio, the faster the company's earnings are expected to grow.) After the crash, p/e's fell to 13, closer to their historical average of 14 to 15. It is reasonable to say, then, that the sudden devaluation in stock prices brought p/e's back to their traditional range.

Fourth, there was a feeling that if this was, in fact, a fatal crisis, we deserved it. The stock market crash followed years of criticism that the United States was living beyond its means: Consumers had been on a credit card binge; government had spent and borrowed itself silly; and business debt had gotten entirely out of hand—indeed, leveraged buyouts were taken to be the symbol of what was wrong with the country. The crash was the long-awaited, and richly deserved, punishment. Or, in the metaphors of the moment, we were paying the piper; we were experiencing the great hangover.

Hence, the market crash seemed to be unlike other crises where Americans could feel victimized. This was not the result of evil Arab oil producers, crafty Japanese mercantilists, or greedy foreign currency traders; no, this was a crisis that could be laid firmly at our door. Feeling guilty and penitent, people could hardly ask their government for a bailout.

And finally—and perhaps most significantly— there was a recognition that there wasn't much the government could do, even if it wanted to. Globalization of the financial markets was an irreversible fact. If the government did something untoward, like reregulate the domestic markets, the world's investors (including Americans) would punish it by taking their money and their business elsewhere.

For this mix of reasons, there was no great consensus for the government to step in and do something about the crash. And it didn't.

The Federal Reserve, which had responded to the liquidity crunch by flooding the economy with money—interest rates dropped briefly to below 5 percent after the crash—went back to its policy of tight money. By the middle of November, interest rates were creeping back up again, the "excess" liquidity had been mopped up.

The commission investigating the crash, known as the Brady Commission, made its report in January 1988. Like all good bureaucratic efforts, the report pointed the finger of blame at everyone. Nonetheless—also like all good bureaucratic efforts—its recommendations were toothless.

Importantly, too, the dollar was allowed to find its own level on the foreign exchange markets. As it was before the crash, the administration was faced with three choices. It could raise interest rates to defend the dollar or employ Baker's tantrum strategy of driving the dollar down steeply or it could let the dollar float. The first two options required the government to intervene in the foreign exchange markets, the third option was laissez–faire—or, as it turned out—laissez–tomber. The administration chose the third and the dollar kept falling. By mid-November, it was at its lowest level against the yen and the mark for the postwar period, down almost 50 percent from its high in February 1985.

So, in the end, the government did very little about the stock market crash. And virtue was its own reward. The rest of the year passed without bad effect. Indeed, the next year, 1988, came and went without a recession. And so did 1989. Growth slowed but continued to be positive, unemployment stayed low and the climb in both interest and inflation rates abated. In November 1989, the economic expansion passed its seven-year mark, making it the longest postwar expansion on record. The stock market crash of 1987 had proved to be quite dramatic but relatively harmless.

The fact that the government was willing to admit its mistake—or, at least, to refrain from additional intervention in the foreign currency markets and to let economic events take their course—was largely responsible for the successful resolution. If government had tried to "fix" the crash, the outcome would not have been so benign.

The stock market crash of 1987 was, in one basic sense, predictable. It is impossible for government to micromanage events in a world of international markets. When the government sat on its hands, the economic climate in the United States was encouraging to global investors. Opportunities in business were created, and taken advantage of, by both domestic and foreign investors. On the other hand, when government intervention—in this case, in the foreign currency markets—looked as if it would exacerbate an already troubled economy, global markets responded as economic interests dictated. Investors dumped the dollar and flew out of stocks.

The bigger lesson is that government intervention in the economy for short-term goals is usually dumb. Such activism begets a counterresponse from economic players, generates uncertainty in everybody else, and is counterproductive. When the Reagan administration returned to its long-term stance of allowing the economy to work things out for itself, things did work out.

2

Unintended Consequences: The Luxury Tax of 1990

W hen I first heard about the tax on luxury boats," says Victor Eubanks, a carpenter, "I said, Yes! Go for it. Why shouldn't rich people pay more?" At least that was his thought back in January 1991. When I talked with him in 1993, he had been laid off from his job at Viking Yachts in New Gretna, New Jersey, for 13 months. He continued, "But then when I saw it was making businesses close down, I said, Wait a minute. People in Washington see a piece of paper with some numbers on it. They don't see the lives they are disrupting."

And "people in Washington"—as Eubanks so politely put it— disrupted a lot of lives in New Gretna with the luxury tax of 10 percent on boat sales over $100,000. Indeed, the luxury tax is a beautiful illustration of how government activism can precipitate unintended consequences: Rich people didn't want to pay the tax; so rich people stopped buying Viking boats, which cost between

$400,000 and $2 million each. Inventories sat on the floor. Too bad for the firm's owners, Bill and Bob Healey. They stopped building and started laying off workers. Too bad for the workers, like Victor Eubanks. In 1990, the firm employed 700 people; in July 1992, it was down to 175, with some workers on reduced hours.

And too bad for the village of New Gretna and for Bass River Township where Viking Yachts is the major employer. According to Richard Bethea, the mayor of Bass River Township, Viking represents almost 8 percent of the township's total tax base. "If they were to suffer a demise," he told me in 1992, "the tax rate would have to go up 7 to 8 percent to cover current services, mostly the elementary and high school." But that's a problem, too. "If I lose $122,000 in taxes, I have to make it up out of some working slob. But some of them are already out of work and delinquent taxes are way up."

The township had to defer plans to buy a new fire truck for the volunteer fire department and it watched the only bank in town close—victim of the cutback in Viking's payroll, which it processed. Mayor Bethea said that on Fridays, payday, traffic used to be so congested on the main street that the township asked the state of New Jersey for a stoplight. They got the stoplight. The luxury tax rendered it unnecessary.

Victor Eubanks' wife, Carol, worked full-time at the 24-hour convenience store. Her hours were reduced when the store cut back its hours because, as people lost their jobs, they started shopping at the cheaper supermarket on weekends. The Eubankses have two small children. Victor had, by his count, applied for over 600 jobs—everything from Burger King to landscaping, dock worker to day care. "I used to earn $9 to $10 an hour. Right now I'd take $5," he said.

Ditto for Linda Hooper, a laid-off fiberglass specialist at Viking. When she first heard about the luxury tax, she liked it. But, then, when she thought about it, she figured if she could afford an expensive boat, she would buy a used one, not subject to the tax, instead of a new one. Then she wondered if others would feel the same way. They did.

Mrs. Hooper was making $11 an hour. She spent the summer of 1992 looking for minimum-wage jobs like waitressing. She said that if she is rehired at Viking, she'll make less than before, but that's okay with her. At least she will be working—she has two children living at home, one with cancer. Mrs. Hooper went to Washington with Bob Healey, chairman of Viking, to testify before Congress about the impact of the tax: "They didn't seem to care, Democrats or Republicans, they weren't worrying about the people," she said.

As an example of the folly of micromanaging the economy, the 1990 luxury tax is almost too classic to be credible. The tax on certain luxury goods was levied to both raise revenue and stick it to rich people. It did neither. Instead, it damaged the lives of a lot of working people.

The immediate reason for the tax was the federal budget deficit. Between 1989 and 1990, the deficit as a share of the economy grew from 3 percent to 4 percent. Since Washington wasn't interested in cutting spending—indeed, spending was zooming out of control—more tax revenue was needed. The result was the budget agreement of 1990—President George Bush's slip of the read-my-lips-no-new-taxes promise. This agreement was hammered out over the summer and fall of 1990 within official Washington.

An initial candidate for raising cash was wine-beer-and-liquor. A nice bump-up in the excise tax seemed like an easy solution. Not only was it a tax on, ahem, sin, but federal taxes on beer and wine, which hadn't been increased since 1951, were very modest. There were two glitches, however. One of the budgeteers was Rep. Richard Gephardt, Democrat of Missouri, whose St. Louis district includes Anheuser-Busch, the people who make Bud. Probably more damaging was the brilliant ad campaign run by the beer lobby. Consider the print ad showing a long, elegant bare arm whose wrist was encircled by a two-inch-wide diamond bracelet and whose manicured fingers rested around a beer can. The copy read: "Riddle: What's the difference between a diamond bracelet and a can of beer? You pay more excise tax on the beer." The ad continued: "Congress eliminated excise taxes on expensive perfumes, fur coats and jewelry. The kinds of things only the wealthy and powerful can afford." And to put an even finer point on the argument: "American's 80 million beer drinkers are responsible, hard-working men and women who already pay more than their fair share."

After that assault, what could the budget brainstormers do but turn to a tax on the rich? Not that there was ever enough money in taxing the rich to make a real dent in the budget deficit. But Washington needed to look as if it were doing something: to furrow its official brow, to roll up its official sleeves and get down to the business of finding some more money, preferably from the diamond-bracelet crowd.

But what kind of tax on the rich? The Bush administration was firm about not increasing marginal income tax brackets. So how about a tax on things that only rich people bought? How about a tax on luxuries? (Ultimately, however, income tax rates on rich people were bumped up by phasing out the personal exemption and limiting itemized deductions. This basically increased top rates to beyond 31.9 percent.)

The country had had a luxury tax—it was levied during World War II and finally repealed in 1965 as part of a law reducing excise taxes. The tax was a 10 percent rate on standard higher-end items like jewelry, watches, sterling silverware, perfume, furs, handbags, luggage, and—to ice the cake—opera glasses and lorgnettes. Secretary of the Treasury Henry Fowler, in urging the repeal before the Senate Finance Committee, had called the tax burdensome and discriminatory; there was also some question of whether it cost more to administer than it collected.

Anyway. Dopey ideas never die in Washington. So the luxury tax was put on a boilerplate list of 70 to 80 tax ideas that hangs around the Treasury Department. In 1990, this list was whipped out and offered to the budgeteers. It was passed around for comment to all sides—Democrats, Republicans, House, Senate, and Executive—10 to 15 times. The first short list to emerge from this round-robin had 30 items, including the luxury tax. Nobody remembers who, exactly, plucked this tax out of the possibilities, but most players, off-the-record, finger Gephardt.

In its first form, the tax was estimated to raise $8.1 billion in revenues over five years (a semiserious number), but that version included electronic products costing more than $1,000. After that provision was dropped—heavy lobbying from the electronics industry—the Joint Committee on Taxation estimated a yield of $1.5 billion over five years (a howlingly small number). The tax took the form of a 10 percent levy on amounts above a threshold: $10,000 for furs, $10,000 for jewelry, $30,000 for autos, $100,000 for boats, and $250,000 for airplanes. There was very little research and almost no discussion of the probable impact of the tax. And there was no chance for public comment.

And thus the luxury tax became part of the budget agreement of 1990, effective January 1, 1991, that popped out of a final weekend of furrowed bipartisan brows at Andrews Air Force Base.

By the summer of 1991, there was plenty of evidence that the tax was backfiring; one story, in the *Wall Street Journal* in June, described how specially equipped vans for the handicapped were considered "luxury" goods because of the added expense in modifying them. Most of the press attention indicated that rich people were not being suckered into buying stuff that required a new 10 percent tariff which sent money into Washington; moreover, industries already hit by the recession, caused in part by the budget agreement, were then being double-whammied to death by its luxury tax provision.

That the tax backfired is clear in retrospect. That official Washington could have anticipated problems, had they paused to give the matter one minute's thought, is also clear.

Yet, in fairness, estimating the impact of a tax is hard going. There is, of course, economic theory that says a tax raises prices and thus discourages purchases. But how many purchases? That depends on price elasticity. If there are no close substitutes for a product, if the product is critical to daily life or consumes a small part of one's budget, then economists call demand for that product "inelastic," which means that people mostly go ahead and buy it anyway, paying the tax. Luxury goods are probably not inelastic, however, because buyers can substitute an untaxed swimming pool or tennis court for a taxed yacht; by definition, luxury goods aren't strictly necessary and they're expensive enough to make even the rich think twice. On the other hand, these goods might be more inelastic than appears at first blush: does a race horse really substitute for a giant diamond engagement ring? Or is a two-week cruise in the Greek islands as satisfying as a mink coat in the winter?

There is also the problem of teasing out the impact of such a tax on the economy versus a specific industry. Taxed industries might swoon, but untaxed industries might get the benefit of the dollars in search of a product. For example, the luxury tax might deck yachts, but untaxed weekend-home sales might boom.

There are also indirect costs to figure, like the added cost of compliance (extra IRS agents and paperwork for sellers). And when the tax discourages purchases and dampens business, there are extra costs from increased unemployment benefits, and costs in the form of decreased personal income tax revenue from laid-off workers and diminished payroll taxes and corporate income taxes from affected industries.

At any rate, it fell to the Joint Committee on Taxation to estimate the revenue yield from the tax. They did and they overestimated. In February 1992, the JCT revised its figures to show revenue from the first year, 1991, at $98 million. Obviously, five years of revenue around $100 million would not get them to the $1.5 billion total-take figure. So the committee made some rosy assumptions about the future, and years two through five show rather large revenue increases (up to $441 million by year five). The committee also figured that administrative costs (the only cost considered) would be $492 million the first year but decline to $202 million in subsequent years.

A reasonable person might pause here to think that the JCT could have done a more credible job—after all, the tax was bound to injure some citizens. Yet, the problems of estimating the impact seem to have defeated even the mighty Government Accounting Office. Responding to a request from several senators and representatives, the GAO issued a report in 1992, which said that the factors affecting the five industries were too "diverse to disentangle" and declined to offer any estimates.

The Republican staff of the Joint Economic Committee, however, met the challenge head-on and, using a somewhat more sophisticated approach, offered a report in 1991 on the impact on three of the affected industries—boats, airplanes, and jewelry. It found that the tax would throw 9,000 people out of work and cost the federal government about $20 million. Other tax experts agreed, but declined to put a specific number to the net loss to the government.

While the numbers debate will probably never be resolved to the penny, there is no doubt that the general result was that the tax cost way more than it raised in revenue. Recognizing that economists are chary of anecdotal evidence (how can we test it?!?) or studies commissioned by lobby groups (are they unbiased!?!), and that journalists have no shame, I offer the results of one journalist's investigation of the impact of the luxury tax made during 1992. Comfortingly for economic theory, the results fall right in line—if you tax something, thereby raising its price, people will buy less of it. If people buy a lot less of it (because the demand for it is very price elastic), the tax might cost more to levy than it generates in revenue. Less comforting was the real life havoc created. Consider:

Autos. This was the luxury tax's big engine of revenue. Almost 90 percent of the take in 1991 came from car sales. But there is an odd thing about the tax. A tax on cars over the threshold price of $30,000 fell hardest on foreign models. Also, of foreign car sales, the burden was borne mostly by European cars (BMW, Jaguar, Mercedes, and Porsche—and Ferrari and Rolls-Royce, of course), rather than Japanese (Lexus and Infiniti), because the average price of a European high-end car was higher than the average high-end Japanese car.

The trade group reports were fairly uniform. Correcting for the recession (and an increase in the gas guzzler tax in 1991), they estimated that the luxury tax resulted in a 20 percent drop in sales.

This pretty much squares with the experience of Tom Nemet of Nemet Motors in Jamaica, Queens. Nemet sells Nissan, Volvo, and Jaguar. It's a third-generation business and he has two sons working with him. With $4 million to $5 million in inventory, Nemet Motors is considered medium to biggish.

I visited Nemet in the spring of 1992. He had already laid off three employees—a 72-year-old woman in accounting and two parts men—and he had mentally scheduled more layoffs for the summer. His sales were down 20 percent, which translated into a 42 percent loss in pretax income. In luxury cars, he sold 15 a month before the stock market crash of 1987; after the crash, he sold eight a month; after the tax he sold one a month. He wasn't sure how much of the downturn was due to the recession—somewhere between 25 and 50 percent—but his margins had shrunk from 10 percent to 5 percent. "I've never had a loss for a whole year in my life," Nemet says; he pauses, "but now I'm scared."

He said his customers were furious about the tax. "Oh, they can afford it, but they won't pay it. They walk out the door." Nemet was eating the tax if it was in the $300-to-$400 range.

In 1991, the IRS informed him that they were sending an agent over for three days to audit his luxury tax account. "I said fine," Nemet remembers. "The woman stayed two hours and left." From January to June, Nemet had only sold four cars subject to the tax.

Fur. The fur business was in deep trouble before the recession and before the luxury tax. Sudden and widespread bankruptcies of department stores and an aggressive animal rights movement had made the retail environment uncertain and cautious. Moreover, the fur industry, with sales of $1.5 billion, is just a teensy blip on the economic screen. And the tax take—mostly on mink and sable coats—was never estimated at more than $3 million a year and was under $1 million in 1991.

So why would official Washington bother? That's the question asked by Jack Pearson, vice president and general manager of Maximilian, which retails through Bloomingdale's. When I saw him in the summer of 1991, he had laid off 20 percent of his staff—salespeople, sales support people, buyers, marketing people, and his own secretary. (During the hour I spent in his tiny, messy office, Pearson apologetically answered his own phone six or seven times.) Half those layoffs he attributed to the recession, half to the luxury tax.

When the tax first went into effect, Pearson got a good lesson in just how elastic the demand for furs is. Each time his salespeople made a sale on a coat over the $10,000 threshold, they explained that they would have to collect the tax. Customers balked—and started to walk away. Salespeople conferred with managers. Managers phoned Pearson. During the heavy buying season, October through March, Pearson got these calls every day. For two months, Pearson refused to absorb the tax. "I 'walked' every single customer out the door," he says.

Then he started to absorb the tax. His margins went from 20 percent to 10 percent. He started to pinch his wholesalers to split the difference. Some of his wholesale manufacturers went overseas to cheaper countries like Greece, Hong Kong, or China. Meaning that more U.S. jobs were lost.

One of Pearson's manufacturers is Jeff Tepper of the Tepper Collections. Tepper is the third generation in the fur business and has resisted going overseas because he doesn't want to lose control over the manufacturing process. He says that Pearson was pinching him, but that in 1992, he made a mink coat, in four styles, for Pearson that would retail for under $10,000. "They are lovely coats, but not the same quality of the $15,000-to-$18,000 coats we used to do for him," he says. "We made six dozen instead of six, so the greater volume will mean less markup." But the pinching hurts; Tepper had laid off half his staff since 1989.

The Fur Information Council believes that between January 1991 and February 1992, 10,000 jobs were lost, but it doesn't offer an apportionment of blame between recession and luxury tax.

Airplanes. Small plane makers had been nibbled thin by a number of negatives before the recession and luxury tax sunk their teeth in: high costs associated with product liability claims, loss of a number of small airports, and elimination of the investment tax credit in 1986. The 10 percent threshold on planes and helicopters over $250,000 was another category not expected to raise much revenue—no more than $4 million a year. Almost 40 percent of the general aviation market represents exports, and the majority of domestic craft are used for business—neither category was subject to the tax.

Still, the tax managed to do a fair amount of damage. Consider Beech Aircraft. Beech is basically the only manufacturer of piston and turboprop aircraft—the two craft that generally comprise the owner-flown market. "The nonbusiness, owner-flown part of our market is devastated," Jim Gregory, director of corporate affairs, tells me a year after the tax was enacted.

Beech is the second largest employer in Kansas, with a payroll of 7,300. In the fall of 1990, before the tax was a sure thing, the company announced plans to hire 500 more people in 1991. But because of the recession, the Gulf War, and the luxury tax, Beech ended up cutting back turboprop production from 133 to 100 a year. In the first year of the tax, Beech figured that lost sales directly attributed to the tax translated into 480 lost jobs. (The typical laid-off worker is highly skilled and usually finds a job at one of the subcontractor firms in the Wichita area, thus bumping off someone else farther down the line.)

According to Gregory, distributors reported back that customers were refusing to buy rather than pay the tax. The only aircraft for which the dealer absorbed the tax was the Bonanza piston where the majority of the price was below the threshold, so a dealer only had to eat $5,000—versus the $380,000 to $400,000 tax on a $2.2 million or $4.2 million King Air turboprop.

In anticipation of the tax, back in the fall of 1990, Beech also stopped work on a new headquarters in Wichita. The materials were already bought and delivered, but the area was paved over to prevent erosion; it became a parking lot.

Jewelry. This is not a big industry—$25 billion to $30 billion—made up mostly of thousands of small stores that are more likely to suffer from a recession than from a tax on stuff over $10,000. High-end sales are dominated by five big firms: Cartier, Tiffany, Van Cleef, Bulgari, and Harry Winston. While these stores were thought to pay 70 percent of the tax, they have foreign outlets and a lot of foreign customers that escape taxation.

The industry group, the Jewelry Coordinating Committee, reported that 15,000 workers were laid off between January 1 and February 1992, "reflecting the bleakest Christmas sales in recent memory" and a bunch of retail bankruptcies. The committee attributed more than half of the 11 percent decline in sales to the tax. Sales on items over the threshold were down 40 percent from January to June 1991.

But talk to one of the big five and the impact seems less dire. Ronald Winston, head of Harry Winston, divided blame 50-50 between the recession and the tax. He laid off 25 of 200 workers during the year and a half after the tax. Winston says that sometimes he'll absorb the tax, but then, he is quick to add, he pays less corporate profits tax. (Winston says he doesn't try to push the tax back to diamond dealers because their margins are too thin.)

The tax on jewelry over $10,000 also had a particularly foolish provision. Say your grandma dies, leaving you a $15,000 diamond ring. If you had wanted to change the setting, the whole package was subject to the tax. Yes, jewelers had to charge customers the tax on the value of the stone they brought in, plus the tax on the value of the mounting.

"As soon as I tell them that, they say 'You're crazy' and walk out the door," says James Gianforte of Continental Jewelers in Washington, D.C. Gianforte couldn't offer to absorb the tax because a typical mounting costs only $500 and the stone a lot more, so the tariff was much higher than the margin he made from the mounting. Gianforte says, "I've never had one single customer sit still for this." His remounting work, which had been 15 percent of his business, was almost down to zero when I spoke with him in the fall of 1992.

Gianforte doesn't sell much jewelry above the $10,000 threshold, so his overall business wasn't affected much. Nonetheless, since his markups are small"—"Our business is so competitive"— he couldn't absorb the tax on new sales over the threshold. He just kissed them off.

Boats. The boating industry—or, at prices over $100,000, one should say the yachting industry—was surely the most outraged and, by most accounts, the most hammered by the luxury tax.

According to its trade group, overall sales of big boats dropped 75 percent and unemployment rose 47 percent in 1991, versus the typical recession experience when sales drop 30 to 40 percent. That translated into the loss of 20,000 to 25,000 jobs, mostly blue collar. The group says that the $7 million in luxury taxes collected in 1991 didn't balance off the lost payroll taxes, so there was a net revenue loss for the government.

The damage was particularly dramatic because almost all big boat builders are privately owned firms and thus lack the financial resources of the large public corporations that build smaller, less expensive boats. Some big boat builders, including the great names, went into bankruptcy (Bertram Yacht and Egg Harbor), while others (Hatteras and Viking) were forced into financial restructuring.

Business at Viking Yachts had grown every year since Bob and Bill Healey bought the firm in 1964, even during recessions, when business usually falls 15 to 20 percent. Nineteen ninety-one was its first year of shrinkage. In 1990, Viking sold 180 boats; in 1991, only 40 boats. In 1990, Viking had 1,300 employees (including 600 in St. Petersburg, Florida); in 1991, at its low point, Viking had 88 workers. Viking ate 100 percent of the tax; it was the only way they could sell a boat.

• • •

To be fair to official Washington, after it was clear—early on—that the tax was backfiring, a fairly large consensus developed for repeal. Nonetheless, despite many attempts, most of the provisions of the tax weren't finally laid to rest until 1993. The tax on autos (remember, it fell mostly on foreign cars) was retained and indexed for inflation.

In short, the luxury tax failed in every respect. Official Washington thought a tax on luxury goods would be a painless and politically correct way to raise revenue. Painless because rich people is where the money is and politically correct because it applied only to expensive goods. How nice! The luxury tax would not only collect money but would do so while achieving a social objective.

Fine. But any economist would have predicted that by taxing something, one is likely to get fewer people to buy it. Indeed, nobody, including the rich, likes to be fleeced. So rich people stopped buying the goods. And the everyday people who produced those goods suffered. Bottom line: The government didn't raise nearly the money it anticipated and it disrupted thousands of lives.

And that's the problem with active government policy—people don't sit still and wait for its consequences to unroll. If they have the choice to evade the consequences, they exercise it. In this case, rich people had a choice, the consequences fell to others to absorb.

3

Regulatory Suffocation: Four Stories from the Front

When Charlie Bacall arrives at his office in the morning, he is very careful about where he hangs up his coat. Very careful. Not because his boss is looking over his shoulder; he's the boss. Not because his secretary is a neatness maniac; she isn't. He is careful because if he hangs his coat next to his lab coat, agents of the federal government can close his office down. Charlie Bacall is a doctor. His practice is regulated by the government.

Invasive government regulation is a direct consequence of the notion that government knows best and that social and economic goals can be achieved by bureaucratic fiat. The drive to regulate began slowly in the 1960s, raced along during the 1970s, held its own during the 1980s, and accelerated in the early 1990s. The result of 30-plus years of bureaucrats with the power to direct events has been the near suffocation of everyday activity for many businesspeople, especially those with small firms.

If that sounds too dire to you, then you are part of the lucky portion of the population that is insulated from this daily intrusion. Your direct brushes with the government are probably confined to specific and discrete events—paying taxes, being licensed to drive a car, or getting a call for jury duty. And although it's hard to think of an industry or profession in which government regulation is absent, the experience for some is more intense than others. If you work for a big employer, for example, the chances are that your job has little to do with government regulation—that is usually the province of other employees in the company; if you work for yourself, however, the government is in your face. The extent of the damage becomes clear when the direct impact of regulation is examined. So here are some real stories of what happens when the government mucks about in the way we do business.

First, I've chosen two doctors. Charles J. Bacall and Roy Levit are small-business people who bear the brunt of the good ideas gone bad embedded in government regulation—cost, daily frustration, and demoralization. I've known Dr. Bacall for many years because I am one of his patients. I know him to be a dedicated physician and not particularly a whiner or a complainer. I don't know Dr. Levit, but he is respected, successful, and was amenable to an interview. Like many doctors, neither is interested in or knowledgeable about business practices or management.

Bacall, 45 years old, became a doctor for predictable reasons: He had an aptitude for science and, preferring people to lab work, chose to be a physician rather than a researcher. But he had other reasons as well. As the child of a poor immigrant family, his father told him more than once: Be your own boss. Bacall says, "My getting a medical education was a way of developing independence in the system, a way of assuring me middle-class status." Did he think it was also a way of getting rich? "Oh, no. When I was training in the 1970s, I thought if I could make $50,000 a year, it would be the best thing that ever happened to me."

Bacall graduated with an M.D. in 1975 from New York Medical College. When I interviewed him, he was an assistant professor of obstetrics, gynecology, and reproductive sciences at Mount Sinai Hospital in New York City, with an appointment at the Mount Sinai School of Medicine. His practice, which he shares with four other doctors, employed three medical assistants, two office managers, and three medical receptionists.

One of his office managers, Linda Wilhelmy, describes her work as "a ton of paperwork and millions of phone calls." She handles patient billing, disability forms, operating room bookings, blood donations, and off-site appointments for consultations. She works from 8:15 A.M. to 6:00 P.M., eating lunch at her desk. That's her job and she likes it, feeling she gets double satisfaction from helping the doctors and their patients.

Bacall's practice is, for New York City, a fairly old-fashioned one. He doesn't, as many of his colleagues do, demand payment for surgery in advance. "We operate on a handshake. If patients can't pay, we assume they are telling the truth." And if they don't pay? "As long as they send some regular, small payment as a gesture of goodwill, we let it go." He doesn't take credit cards. "It doesn't seem professional," he says.

Three years ago, Bacall's office spent $30,000 for a computerized billing system. This concession to modern medical practice was late in coming but finally necessary because to bill the old way meant longer waits from insurance companies and the federal government for reimbursement.

It is clear that the office is set up as a business out of necessity and not as a primary object. "There's a fine line between medicine and business. We can't make it feel like a business to patients, but still we want to get paid," says Wilhelmy.

While Bacall doesn't take Medicaid patients at his office, he does treat them through his hospital as an attending doctor two days a month and on call one or two nights a month. The hospital bills Medicaid in his name but keeps the money.

As for Medicare patients, given the nature of his practice, he has a relatively large share. Many are patients who started coming to the office in the 1940s; although the doctors who treated them are now retired, Bacall keeps them on because he likes them and views them as a legacy of the founders of the practice. (They are called the "fountain pen ladies" because their early record entries are written in fountain pen.)

On a 24-patient day, five will be obstetrics, 15 will be gynecological, and four will be fountain pen ladies. When Bacall started practicing medicine, Medicare reimbursement rates were comparable to costs. Now, they cover 80 percent of "allowable charges." Bacall charges, on average, $140 for a routine checkup; Medicare allows $47.63. He figures that he loses money on every Medicare patient. Not just on the dollar rate, but the time spent. While he could be spending an average of 15 minutes with a private patient, Medicare patients take about twice that long—both to undress and dress and because they have multiple complaints. "Their visit is a very important part of their day, their week," says Bacall, "so they can't be rushed and I don't want to rush them."

There is, of course, no way to see Medicare patients at a reasonable rate—even if they are rich and wish to reimburse him privately. "If I know they are over 65, I can only charge them the Medicare rates, and these rates are capped. No reasonable fee-for-service is allowed. The wisest business decision I could make would be to stop taking Medicare patients," says Bacall. Many of his colleagues already have.

But that's hardly Bacall's biggest headache. Of the migraine variety, there are two. The first is the Clinical Laboratory Improvements Amendments of 1988, which covers in-office testing. Obviously, as both Bacall and Wilhelmy agree, in-office tests should be performed under certain standards and by qualified people. But, they argue, although CLIA standards may have started as a good idea, they quickly have become unnecessarily nitpicky.

For example, CLIA directs that only doctors may peer into a microscope—no matter that medical assistants have been trained to do so. About 90 percent of complaints can be diagnosed under a microscope, an inexpensive and quick procedure. But if doctors don't have the time, the microscope is either bypassed, resulting in a higher percentage of incorrect decisions, or the slides are sent out to a lab, which costs five to ten times more than in-office and takes several days.

Ditto for in-office blood testing. It's an easy procedure, and the machines that perform the tests are very accurate, but since CLIA requires two controls to be run once a day on each item—hemoglobin and cholesterol, in this case—blood testing has become expensive and time-consuming. Bacall has compromised by limiting the days on which his office does blood tests.

CLIA also requires an enormous amount of paperwork. Everything must be logged; for instance, the temperature of the refrigerator and freezer must be monitored and recorded every day, as must a list of patients having tests performed, a list of all control serums and their expiration dates. The office must also have a cleaning schedule for the lab, notes on how problems are taken care of, and a typed procedures manual stating how tests are to be performed—the manufacturers' manuals are not enough.

Bacall's office was checked by a CLIA agent last July, at his expense. The three-hour visit of one agent cost the office $1,000, payable to the federal government. If the agent had found anything out of line, they would have been fined, in addition to the inspection fee.

The net is that an increasing portion of Wilhelmy's salary and office budget is being spent on satisfying the demands of government surveillance and a decreasing number of tests are performed in-office because they are no longer economically viable. Even after cutting back on in-office testing, Wilhelmy figures that following CLIA requirements takes a half hour of her day, every day.

A second migraine comes from regulations by the Occupational Safety and Health Administration. They are initially felt by Wilhelmy, who says it takes weeks of research to figure out just what OSHA wants when it issues guidelines. The last big issuance required, among other things, the office to purchase a bunch of signs to alert people that smoking, eating, or drinking were not allowed in the lab area; the purchase of special cleaning substances to mop up spills; the designation of a separate space as an "eye wash station" in case anybody gets something in his or her eye during a procedure; and the purchase of separate refrigerators for certain items, clearly marked "BIOHAZARD: No food or drink in this refrigerator." Anything that might be touched by a doctor when examining a patient must be wrapped in plastic, including the examining light, which is sheathed in a sort of condom that must be changed after every patient.

Beyond the frustration and expense of having the government micromanage his office practices, Bacall resents having his treatment decisions second-guessed. "There is a layer, often a large bureaucracy—a government agency or some insurance company—interposed between me and my patient. I have to justify the treatment I know is right. I spend a lot of unreimbursed time on the phone calling and arguing with these gatekeepers."

The basic story is the same for Dr. Levit: Government regulation constitutes a daily frustration and intrusion in the way he practices medicine.

Levit, 53, is an ophthalmologist specializing in retinal surgery. He got his degree at the University of Texas and began private practice in 1975 in El Paso, Texas. He works with two other doctors. The office employs 14 people; six devote full time to the business side of things—an office manager, three clerks to handle insurance and collections, a receptionist and a transcriber (because all chart notes are dictated). Levit spends, on average, an hour a day with the office manager.

Like Bacall, he's had to computerize his billing system—at a cost of $40,000 over the past five years—but he still waits, and waits, for reimbursement. "One of the reasons we computerized was to speed reimbursement, but now that the majority of physicians file electronically, the government has extended payment time to precomputer levels by rejecting valid claims over and over again," says Levit.

Levit sees on average 30 patients a day, five to seven of them are new, the rest are there for follow-up treatments. He sees both Medicare and Medicaid patients. He says that everybody is treated the same medically, but the demands imposed by government insurance means patients are dealt with differently: "For example, Medicaid will only pay for one test per visit, so if we want to be reimbursed, we have to make the patients come in three or four times just to perform the minimum number of necessary tests," he says. That is, if the patient lives nearby; for those beyond 150 miles, Levit just does all the tests in one visit—and loses his reimbursement.

Levit's main regulatory nightmare is the Americans with Disabilities Act, especially since many syndromes involve both eye and ear impairment. Before the act, he felt able to communicate with hearing-impaired people by gestures or through writing; now, he must pay $50 an hour for a professional signer to accompany them. In the case of Medicaid, which reimburses $8 for the entire office visit, he is out $42 right off the bat. He reckons that this requirement costs him $200 to $300 a month. (He lucked out on another ADA requirement, however. The arms on his six examining chairs can be removed, so he didn't have to replace them—at $5,000 a pop—to accommodate the grossly overweight.)

Now, all these niggles, taken separately, don't sound like such a big deal. And maybe they're not. And maybe they aren't such a big deal when taken all together. Certainly, both Bacall and Levit earn very good livings despite the regulatory overload and the reimbursement shortfalls. And, certainly, both know doctors who actually make the system work for them—a polite way of saying that some of their colleagues are making out like banshees.

But the effect of all the niggles goes well beyond time and cost and paperwork. A bigger burden hits job satisfaction. Although Bacall is responding rationally to increasing regulation—by cutting back on procedures, hiring two full-time office managers to handle the paperwork and regulatory requirements, and battling the gatekeepers—these responses limit the way he practices medicine. And leave him demoralized. "Part of me likes what I am doing," says Bacall. "It's hard to see myself doing anything different. But I am 45 years old and I feel like a dinosaur. I'm on the top of the list of being extinct."

Levit echoes this sentiment. He says that until six years ago, he never considered patients from a financial point of view and that it's hard to accept the new realities: "Younger doctors won't have as much difficulty adjusting to increased regulation and thinking about remuneration, but I feel outmoded in a way—abused may be a better term—it's hard to learn new habits." On the other hand, Levit is also more defiant. "Nobody is going to force me out of private practice. I like helping people with vision problems; I want to continue doing it," he says. "I'm going to pay close attention to the rules and learn to work within the system." Does he feel diminished by playing the game? "Of course I do," he snorts.

Bacall says that when his colleagues get together now, the talk focuses on discontents and often runs to retirement—remember, these are people in their 40s—but they feel boxed in. They can't retire gracefully, cutting back their patient load, because the fixed costs of running an office are so high—computers, regulatory compliance, malpractice insurance, and so forth. Bacall, who says he works, on average, 70 hours a week, feels he can't wind down his practice. "I have three children; so far, not one of them wants to go into medicine and I'm not unhappy about that. In the last 20 years, there have been so many changes, there isn't the same level of career satisfaction," he says.

Granted, medical doctors are probably feeling unusually touchy these days. But listen to two other people in what are more traditionally considered small businesses. Again, both are successful and not prone to pessimism and complaint. And, as with most small business people, they are risk takers who have built a business from the bottom up.

Charlie Palmer has just the kind of history that people are referring to when they talk about the United States being the land of opportunity, and he is just the kind of person that people admire when they talk about the rewards of hard work and talent. Palmer is the owner of one of New York City's best and most fashionable restaurants; he is also a chef with a reputation for innovative American cuisine. And he did it all himself.

Palmer was born in a small town in New York State called Smyrna. During summers and after school, he worked in various restaurants, starting as—what else?—a dishwasher. He liked the work just fine but didn't consider cooking as a career; he thought he would play pro football. (He's a big, fierce-looking guy, at 6 feet 3 inches, 250 pounds.) He didn't actually decide to become a chef until he graduated from high school. He then spent two years at the Culinary Institute in Hyde Park, New York, and came straight to New York City. He rented an apartment in Hell's Kitchen for $50 a month and had his car stolen.

Palmer spent the next several years working at some of New York City's nicer restaurants—like Côte Basque, where he began as a butcher. He also had a bunch of second jobs—like making pastry at La Petite Marmite. By working two jobs, 16 hours a day, he gradually expanded his expertise. And he came to realize that the restaurant business was "strictly a business; the more you put into it, the more you get out of it."

When Palmer finally made his first trip to France, he went right to its gastronomical center, Lyon, and worked in a very famous three-star restaurant. He spent every cent he earned eating at good restaurants. "In France, I really realized what was going on—there, they live for food."

Back in New York City, there was no stopping him. After four years as head chef at the River Café, another important restaurant, he was confident that he could be successful as both a businessman and a chef. So, in 1988, along with two partners (whom he later bought out) Palmer started Aureole.

In a city where the experience of eating is as important as eating itself, restaurants are "designed" by professionals. Not for Palmer. "I wanted to choose the way it looked," he says; he chose the neighborhood (Upper East Side), the building (a brownstone), the ambience (low-key), the place settings (simple), and the flower arrangements (spectacular). "I did sheetwork, I sanded floors, hey! I even did woodwork."

The restaurant, which seats 90 to 100 people, is open for lunch five days a week, dinner six days. It ain't cheap. The fixed-price lunch is $32, dinner is $59. Palmer employs 68 people, including 21 cooks, maîtres d'hôtel, waiters, cashiers, bartenders, and bookkeepers, some of whom are part-time.

Palmer gives new meaning to the term "hands on," saying, "I am the manager and chef—and dishwasher when somebody doesn't show up." And he is also in the restaurant whenever food is served, taking vacations only when it is closed. During the first two years, Palmer worked from 7:00 A.M. to 1:00 A.M.

On the day I visited him, he was wrestling with "just another hassle" over a recently purchased creamery in Peekskill, New York. Palmer figured that since this country makes so much dairy produce, it shouldn't be all that difficult to make the best-quality butter, cream, and cheese.

The creamery applied to the U.S. Department of Agriculture for all the necessary approvals, got most of them, and then started marketing its cream, butter, chocolate butter, and four types of cheeses to restaurants and specialty food stores. The cream is called "clabbered cream"—an old-fashioned term used by farmers. Three months after the creamery started distribution, the USDA decided to withhold its regulatory approval of the labeling, saying that the word "clabbered" implies the cream was made "in a home."

Palmer was trying to decide what to do, and he was vastly good-humored about it. Perhaps because that was just the problem du jour—he has been hassled by government regulations from the start. Consider Palmer's most exasperating brush with government regulation: Several years ago, as he tells it, a guy came into the restaurant at 9:00 P.M., which was right in the middle of dinner service, and flashed a badge from the Environmental Protection Agency. He told Palmer that he would have to shut down his kitchen exhaust system because there was a complaint that its noise level was above the EPA standard. The restaurant was full.

Palmer explained that if he shut off the exhaust system in the middle of making 100 dinners, the temperature would rise so fast that the fire extinguishing system—38 jets that spew white fire retardant all over the kitchen—would be set off. The EPA agent said, "Shut it down or I'll arrest you," and called the police. Palmer shut it down, the heat in the kitchen skyrocketed, the fire extinguishing system went off and ruined everything in the kitchen.

The cops arrived before Palmer could punch the guy out. Instead, he went from table to table, apologizing and explaining that there would be no dinner that night.

Palmer lost $10,000 in dinners, was fined $1,750 for a noise violation, spent $26,000 to correct the violation, and paid about $60,000 in legal fees. He also endured two visits a week from the EPA for the next six months.

What does he make of this experience? Palmer's response is put mildly, but his message is discouraging. "Regulations don't promote small business growth; they don't help small business to prosper." Is he happy? "It's better than working for someone else," he says.

And, finally, there is James Spradley, Jr., 39 years old. He looks like the Brooks Brothers notion of a corporate lawyer—sandy hair, square jaw, and glinty eyes. And he does business like a corporate lawyer, hiding a crafty intelligence under a seamless layer of good manners. But he's not a lawyer. Never even thought about it. Spradley runs a candy company in Nashville, Tennessee.

Spradley, who got an M.B.A. from the University of Chicago, always wanted to manage a business. Two years after he graduated, he got his wish when he persuaded his father, a retired businessman, to come in with him and buy the Standard Candy Company. The company wasn't exactly hot. It had sales of $2.5 million from a handful of products, notably something called a Goo-Goo Cluster—a roundish bar of peanuts, marshmallow, caramel, and milk chocolate.

That was in 1982. With very little capital, but through what Spradley calls "enormous amounts of energy," the company expanded its products (introducing the Goo-Goo Supreme, a cluster made with pecans instead of peanuts), increased its production, and enlarged its scope. In 1985, Spradley bought another not-so-hot company called Stuckey's—a firm making candy for about 100 roadside shops, mostly in the South, with sales of about $7 million.

When I spoke with him, the combined operations were selling about $35 million annually. Spradley is, obviously, a success. But has his dream come true? Is Spradley managing? "When I graduated from business school, I thought managing a company meant I'd be out selling, doing capital analysis on the purchase of new equipment, managing employees, and developing marketing plans. Instead, half my time is paperwork," he says. While he doesn't blame that directly on government-generated tasks ("I can ask someone else to do it . . ."), he says that regulatory considerations are creeping into every decision he makes.

The firm has to make sure employees are American citizens; although he is forbidden to ask potential employees questions based on race, country of origin, or sex, he then has to file papers on all applicants on their race, sex, and national origin. "We are not supposed to ask, but we are supposed to know." He shrugs. Standard occasionally is asked to collect money from an employee by the courts—garnishments for child support, alimony, or payments to a bankruptcy trustee. Failure to handle this paperwork correctly could result in the company being held liable for the entire amount owed by the employee.

As a food manufacturer, the government agency that Spradley mostly deals with is the Food and Drug Administration. He says, "The FDA is not in our face, it just sneaks up and makes us do something we hadn't planned on and costs a lot."

For instance? Nutritional labeling. In 1992, the FDA mandated that by 1994, all processed foods carry labels describing nutritional value, thus making Standard Candy's packaging obsolete. The company needed new artwork, new printing plates, and a nutritional analysis of its products. Spradley estimates the cost of retooling, depending on the product, at $4,000 to $10,000—for a total of over $150,000. It also meant that $250,000 worth of old packaging held in inventory was unusable for sale in the United States.

There are also the seemingly endless small irritations. "The FDA is constantly outlawing something, so we are constantly having to change ingredients," Spradley said. For example, rules regulating Red Dye No. 2 have changed three times in six years.

A second, more indirect, source of frustration comes from the U.S. Department of Agriculture. Two major ingredients in Spradley's manufacturing process—peanuts and sugar—are highly regulated by the government. Both must be purchased domestically for domestically marketed products. Fine, except domestic peanuts, some of which are grown under a quota system in which the government guarantees purchase, cost two times more than nonquota peanuts. Ditto for sugar, where the world price is two-thirds of the U.S. price.

Because of these two artificially high prices, it costs Standard 15 percent more for raw materials for the U.S. market than it does for exports to Mexico and Europe, where nonquota peanuts and non-U.S. sugar are used. "We pass the increased cost on to our customers," says Spradley, "but the whole exercise is exasperating and requires a significant amount of record keeping."

And then there is just the plain old exasperation over good-hearted government regulations that can have hard-hearted impact. Under the Americans with Disabilities Act, his plants are required to lower the curbs to accommodate people in wheelchairs. Fine. But as Spradley points out, "This is a good thing for people in wheelchairs, but it is heck on blind people, who trip when they can't find a raised curb."

Spradley displays a characteristic businessperson's split personality. On the one hand, he feels that increasing government interference in the marketplace will "soon make the United States as unproductive as France or Germany," but about his own business, he is optimistic. He has two daughters. He hopes that someday both will run the Standard Candy Company.

All four of these businesspeople are coping, to be sure. Each understands that the goals of many regulations are desirable—whether they are to set high standards, ensure safe conditions, enhance the quality of life, or provide equal opportunity. Unfortunately, in trying to achieve these goals, regulation has proved ham-handed and heavy-footed. The problem is that we ask the government to do what it cannot do without establishing huge, unresponsive, and often irresponsible bureaucracies that suffocate daily economic activity. All four of these small business people can be forgiven for wishing that the government would get off their backs.

Part II

Why Government Is So Big and Busy

4

First Step: Bad Ideas

As part I demonstrates, government interference in the economy can generate uncertainty in the private sector, produce unintended consequences that range from very harmful to mildly annoying, and cause regulatory gridlock that saps productivity.

Nonetheless, the idea behind government activism has proved to be powerfully attractive, especially during the last 35 years. And it has kept its appeal despite the fact that it also has had disastrous effects on the broader economy. The next two sections try to explain both the theoretical appeal of an activist government and how it created the problems we are trying to solve today.

The notion that government could micromanage the economy, that active policy could engineer desirable social and economic goals, had a respectable start in the Keynesian policies that came to Washington during the Kennedy administration.

In fingering the Kennedy administration, I am trying to avoid the usual economic historian's approach of running the story line back as far as the written word. A truly serious practitioner of my craft, for example, would find antecedents for government management of economic matters back in the Navigation Acts of the 1650s and 1660s, which set up Great Britain as a great mercantile empire. But in avoiding the sweep-of-history approach, I am also ignoring the important and relevant stage setting that went on during the Great Depression and World War II. So, here follows a quick account of what was going on before the main act started.

It is hard to overestimate the impact of the Great Depression of the 1930s on the national conscience. It was traumatic and shattering. From the Depression's start in 1929 to its trough in 1933, almost a quarter of the population was unemployed and economic activity shrunk by a fifth. And the fact that most of the relevant world had followed the United States into depression by 1931 compounded the sense that something was very, very wrong.

The standard policy response to crisis at that time was minimal. Most policy makers and opinion mongers thought that such crises were inherent to the system, would work themselves out, and that the government should not interfere with this adjustment process. Accordingly, President Herbert Hoover gave priority to state, local, and private efforts, but was against enlisting the federal government. (Back then, the federal role in the economy was tiny: In 1929, federal spending was under 3 percent of economic activity versus over 24 percent today.) During the presidential campaign of 1932, Hoover argued that the Democrats would weaken capitalism by expanding government spending and interfering in the private sector. His critique fell on deaf ears. Most people had lost faith in "automatic adjustments." They wanted a take-charge government.

Not that there was agreement on what, exactly, such an activist government would do. One view, put forward with increasing power, came from the British economist John Maynard Keynes, who early on wanted President Roosevelt to vastly increase spending on public works. But Roosevelt was not interested. While the Roosevelt administration was activist, no question, it was not Keynesian. On balance, despite its public works spending, its policies were only moderately expansionary. Like Hoover, Roosevelt felt that budgets ought to be balanced.

Yet, there was one aspect of Roosevelt's policy that did become part of U.S. Keynesianism: an emphasis on redistributing income. The New Deal did—in the then-fashionable phrase—"increase purchasing power" for the poor, the old, workers, and farmers. Roosevelt also allowed the government to intrude on other parts of the economy by expanding its regulatory reach.

At any rate, Roosevelt did not spend his way out of the Depression. Although government spending reached 7 percent of the economy in 1933, rose to 10 percent for a while, and then hit 16 percent in 1941, a close look yields little evidence that his policies had much impact. Once the economy touched bottom in 1933, the pace of the recovery was, by historical standards, normal. Unfortunately, that pace was not brisk enough for an economy that had fallen so far. It took four years for output to regain pre-Depression levels.

Unemployment had dropped to 14 percent by 1937, but a recession in 1937–38, during which the economy shrunk by 5 percent, bounced unemployment back to 19 percent in 1938 and 17 percent in 1939. The unemployment rate stayed above 10 percent until 1941 and it wasn't until the end of 1942, when the country was fighting World War II, that the economy was fully employed. This has prompted many economic historians to argue, correctly, that Roosevelt did not bring the country out of the Depression, World War II did.

The war did do several other things, however. The boom reminded people of how widespread and satisfying the benefits of a healthy economy were. Coupled with the kind of can-do spirit generated by winning the war came the notion that government could and ought to make full employment a goal.

Thus, the postwar period saw a radical change in how people thought about the responsibilities and capabilities of government. The combination of the profound misery of the Great Depression, the Roosevelt administration's activism, and the happy experience with state planning in World War II made people more friendly to the notion of bigger government. The most visible symbol of the changed attitude toward government responsibility was the Employment Act of 1946 that gave the federal government responsibility for the health of the economy and for low unemployment. The act also created the Council of Economic Advisers, a group of economists who were to function as personal swamis to the president.

In the late 1940s and early 1950s, economic policy debates focused on two questions: how to dampen business cycles and what role government should have in encouraging production. The debates came—inelegantly—under the heading "countercyclical policies aimed at stabilization." From 1945 to 1960, both the Truman and Eisenhower administrations felt that government ought to moderate business ups and downs—by which they meant that government ought to cushion the downs and limit the ups—especially because the economy experienced four recessions: a slight one in 1949, a bigger one in 1954, a medium one in 1958, and a small droop in 1960.

But although their goals were the same, policy seesawed between two economic approaches. For the Truman administration, the emphasis was on active government. It felt that a fully employed economy could be achieved through government policies to goose up consumption spending. The Eisenhower administration, however, rejected constant meddling or creating jobs. Its emphasis was on cutting federal spending, eventually cutting taxes, and balancing the budget. In other words, Democrats preferred government management of the economy and Republicans cleaved to private enterprise.

Then came 1961. And the seesaw tipped decisively: The blueprint for government activism was drawn during the Kennedy administration, the house was built during the Johnson administration. Since the country could have continued under the old doctrine of balanced budgets and modest government involvement in the economy, it's worth a rather long look at just what happened in the 1960s.

The short answer is that several elements came together: eight past years of what was thought to be indifferent economic growth under an accepted orthodoxy; an untried but seductive heterodoxy; an energetic bunch of true believers in that new doctrine; a medium-intelligent president who was the proverbial blank slate in economic matters; and, subsequently, amazingly good luck in the global and national economies.

The economic record was good during the 1950s. Despite several recessions, real growth had averaged 4 percent a year. However, several other economies—those of the Soviet Union, Germany, and Japan—were growing twice as fast as the United States. There was a feeling that the United States could do better and should do better—particularly since unemployment was considered to be high (at 7 percent) when the Kennedy administration came into office.

The heterodoxy, dubbed the New Economics by the press, was not really new. Keynes had established it in his classic work, *The General Theory of Employment, Interest and Money,* published in 1936. And Keynesianism, as it's more properly known, had been gaining ground in university economics departments, particularly on the East Coast, since the 1940s; Paul Samuelson's textbook, *Economics*, had been bringing Keynesianism to waves of college students since its publication in 1948. (Including me. It was my introduction to economics, and I still remember its tone of utter self-confidence and thrilling suggestion of revealed insight.)

At any rate, U.S.-style Keynesianism represented a new approach to economic policy. It advanced several radical arguments: business cycles were not inevitable; deficit spending was quite okay; growth was more important than stable prices; full employment was a reasonable goal; and the dollar could be devalued—or even severed from the price of gold—without risk.

The seductive element, of course, was its promise that the government could fine-tune the economy to produce year after year of economic growth. This required the government to remain in constant motion, manipulating taxes and spending and interest rates to keep up the demand for things: more cars, more steel, more jobs, more salaries, more houses, more televisions, and more factories. This ceaseless tinkering also promised a bonus, something called the multiplier effect, wherein a boost in government spending or a cut in taxes would expand the economy by a multiple of the initial change in spending or taxes. Talk about big bang for a buck . . . !

Say the economy looked a little droopy. The government could race to the rescue, motoring out money either in the form of spending on public housing or transportation or by cutting personal income taxes. This would not only keep demand strong but also would plump up the economy by numbers far greater than the initial boost. Or say that the economy looked a little overheated. Then the government could apply the brakes, absorbing money from the economy, by either cutting its spending or raising taxes. Just a little pressure would be enough to slow things significantly.

But how does the government know when the economy is not performing up to snuff or is, on the other hand, over-snuff? How does it figure the magnitude of the adjustment it must make? After all, too much stimulus or restraint might push the economy into inflation or recession. Keynesians answered these crucial questions with the invention of three tools of analysis—the Phillips curve, the production gap, and the full-employment budget surplus.

The Phillips curve is supposed to show the relationship between the unemployment rate and the inflation rate. That is, it shows a trade-off between the two where higher inflation should mean lower unemployment and lower inflation should mean higher unemployment. During the Kennedy era, the ideal trade-off was thought to be 4 percent unemployment and 2 percent inflation. (Unemployment of 4 percent was taken to be full employment—the best the economy could do without exciting inflation.)

The second tool, the production gap, is best understood as a graph. On the vertical axis is a dollar number for all the goods and services produced by the economy, known as gross national product; on the horizontal axis are the relevant years. Two lines are plotted. One line represents the actual GNP achieved for every year and one line represents the potential GNP (an estimate of what would have been achieved if the economy had been operating "perfectly"). The gap is the difference between the two lines; that is, if potential GNP is above actual GNP, then the gap means the economy is not operating at its potential and expansionary government policies are called for; if, on the other hand, actual GNP is above potential GNP, then the gap shows that the economy is overheating and a contractionary government policy is indicated. (Note that either way, some sort of government action is appropriate.)

Obviously, the calculation of potential GNP is key. It's based on what the economy can theoretically produce with full employment. The 1962 *Economic Report of the President,* the economic bible of the Kennedy administration, has a gap chart that shows potential GNP as a trend line of 3.5 percent annual growth rate, with actual GNP below it at an annual growth rate of about 2.3 percent. Needless to say, that difference creates a rather menacing-looking gap.

The third tool, the full-employment budget surplus/deficit, is an estimate of how the federal budget would look if employment were at full-employment level, or if the economy were operating at its potential. Thus, while the actual budget may be in deficit, the full-employment budget could show a surplus. Policy makers were instructed to pay attention to the full-employment budget—if it showed a surplus, then policy was too contractionary, even if the actual federal budget had a deficit.

And thus did these three notions provide a guide for government action. Now, none of these tools was scientifically determined or proven. But they were very, very useful in arguing against the old doctrine of balanced budgets and government laissez-faire. They at once put the old economics on the defensive. (What? Your administration is running a full-employment budget surplus? You're strangling the economy!! My goodness—you have a big GNP gap. You are holding the country back! Heavens to Betsy—unemployment is over 6 percent and you have zero inflation. You are keeping people unemployed! Shame!)

Indeed, no longer could administrations point with pride to stable prices or a budget surplus; these very things became malign and suspicious. Under Keynesian economics, full employment and snappy growth became the chief goals and any government that wasn't going all out to achieve them was not doing its job. Crucially, of course, doing its job came to mean deficit spending. As long as there was a gap—a shortfall in actual growth from potential growth—then government ought to undertake stimulative measures. If that meant running an actual budget deficit by increasing spending or decreasing taxes, hey! that's the point.

Keynesians also argued that there was only one role for the Federal Reserve—to supply the economy with enough money to keep interest rates low and thus economic activity humming. In other words, Keynesian policies were concerned with the fiscal side of things—taxation and government spending—while monetary policy was thought to be a no-brainer.

So here was a body of thought that was radically different and essentially untried, although it had been enticing academics for 25 years. What remained was to try it out. The New Economics was new in that it represented the first time that Keynesians actually got their hands on the levers of policy.

5

Second Step:
Bad Ideas in Practice

The Keynesian shock troops were bunkered in Kennedy's Council of Economic Advisers. The first economists to go to Washington were, most notably, Walter Heller, Kermit Gordon, James Tobin, Robert Solow, and Arthur Okun. Paul Samuelson was offered a post on the Council but declined, preferring to stay at MIT. He remained an important adviser nonetheless.

In many ways, these Keynesians were alike. They had vivid memories of the Great Depression; they were liberals; most had supported Adlai Stevenson for president. More important, they felt they knew something the older generation of economists didn't know. They felt they were massively more skilled, theoretically and mathematically. Richard Nelson, a staff member of the Council, says, "As economists we had a we-are-wonderful sort of feeling. We had enormous self-confidence and a strong belief that we knew better than other people. We were full of the desire to save the world with economics."

Robert Solow's recollection of why he went to Washington is emblematic. Late one night, in January 1961, before Kennedy's inauguration, Solow was in bed when the phone rang. It was Walter Heller, James Tobin, and Kermit Gordon. They asked Solow to come down to Washington from MIT to join them on the Council.

"My first words were, Why are you up so late at night? I didn't want a job that would make me stay up so late," says Solow. He went back to bed and said to his wife, "Why on earth would I want to do a thing like that for?" He goes on to say, "My wife said that she had been listening to me gripe for the whole Eisenhower administration about its awful economic policy and that maybe I ought to consider putting my money where my mouth was." Solow looks elfish: "I knew I was licked," he says. He called back the next day and accepted a staff position.

Each of the Kennedy Councilites I interviewed said pretty much the same thing. There was a feeling that they were pioneers against the retro world. They speak of enormous esprit de corps, of a sense of mission. But they speak with diffidence, modesty, and irony—although the irony has come with the passage of time. They were all smarter than smart, they were itching to strut their stuff and to save the world from economic ignorance.

They were a moment just waiting to happen.

At the center was Walter Heller, the chairman of the Council. Heller, who died in 1987, appears to have been one of those larger-than-life figures. His colleagues, describing him some 30 years later, seem to have perfect recall. They talk of late nights, endless bull sessions, torrents of memos, Heller blabbing into the phone to the press, Heller hanging around the White House by day and the Council office by night. They remember with relish how he trounced the conservatives over at the Treasury Department and spread the gospel of "modern economics."

The economists did, in fact, bring modern economics to the world. They changed the way people thought about the role of government and they changed the way people thought about economics. They brought a whole new language and culture to policy. Perhaps the most famous phrase in the new vocabulary, "fine tuning," was coined by Heller. It summed up their approach to policy and injected their brand of activism with the aura of sophistication and certainty. It was also the phrase that later came in for ridicule and disapproval.

The notion conveyed by fine tuning is that the economy is like a car: Not only can economists, working through the government, get the car up and running, but they can tinker with its engine and steering to produce a swifter, smoother, more efficient machine.

Tinkering is the key. The economists wanted to avoid making big changes in policy. They wanted to be able to respond quickly. "We wanted to stabilize part of the environment by making frequent, small adjustments," says Solow. "In olden times, a radio had two tuning knobs, one which would get you from one end of the band to the other, and the other inside, that one was called fine tuning." Solow doesn't think it unfair to describe that as what came to be known as fine tuning, but his colleagues are dismissive, not only of the term, but of Heller for uttering it. Samuelson said Heller came to regret it because it was "inappropriate." He says, "It was made to sound pretentious and exact in a way that economics can't be."

Whatever the niceties of the debate, fine tuning created a lot of mischief. Beyond the fact that it didn't work, constant government to-ing and fro-ing destabilized the economic climate, making it difficult for people to make decisions. Solow now says "We probably did not give adequate weight to the importance of a stable decision-making environment."

But that comes later.

For now, imagine the excitement in the Keynesian camp when Heller appeared on the cover of *Time* magazine on March 3, 1961. The story offered an intelligent account of Keynesianism, describing Heller as "seething with drive and energy," "earnest," and "impressive." Of the New Economics, *Time* says it is "a new, cheerful economics" versus the old, dismal kind.

Time instructed its readers that "Kennedy's economists hold the Federal Government responsible because it did not act with sufficient vigor to get the U.S. out of the 1958 recession. In the long run they would run the risk of mild inflation—and, if necessary, even impose controls to keep it mild—to guarantee continued growth and full employment. But more important their theories range to the level of ethical national choices. They hold that the quality of American life—the level of education, the extent of unemployment and poverty—is a prime responsibility of government. Thus they see taxes and budgets not as evil or good in themselves, but as instruments for doing the things they think government ought to do."

The article ended by warning that Congress, especially the House, would be reluctant to give the administration all the extra money the programs needed. "The House's wariness reflects a widespread public wariness towards the new economic goals," *Time* said.

Not only were Congress and the voters chary, so was the new president. Indeed, Kennedy's 1961 plan to counter the recession was strictly Eisenhower. Although the Keynesians urged a tax cut or increased spending, Kennedy made a firm commitment to a balanced budget.

Kennedy started out as an economic conservative for various reasons. First, it was what he knew. As most of his advisers admit, Kennedy's economic literacy was strictly lowest common denominator. Says Tobin, "Kennedy didn't know any economics. He had gone through the campaign without knowing anything." Second, his tiny election margin made him politically cautious; he didn't want to be seen losing battles to conservatives in Congress. Too, his narrow presidential victory was scarcely a mandate for a bunch of activist programs. Third, Kennedy's doctrine of sacrifice (ask-not-what-your-country-can-do-for-you) didn't fit with tax cuts and big spending increases. As Heller told interviewers some years later: "Tax cuts were ruled out because of the sacrifice doctrine. He had told me . . . 'I know you're for a tax cut. I can't come in on a platform of sacrifice and the very first thing hand out tax cuts to people. That just won't wash.'" All in all, as Paul Samuelson remembers, Kennedy began life in office as "an extremely cautious person. He tested the ice in front of him all the time."

The economists were down but not out. Heller had Kennedy's ear and began to talk in it regularly, pounding away at the theme that faster growth and lower unemployment could be achieved by enlightened government action.

The economists' first big break came with the Berlin Wall crisis in the summer of 1961. Kennedy had decided to ask for a tax increase to finance a budget add-on for the emergency mobilization. His reasoning was conventional: It appeared that the budget deficits for 1961 and 1962 would be higher than originally thought, and additional defense spending would only make things worse. Too, the developing recovery eliminated the need for deficit financing, which, along with the increase in spending, threatened price and wage stability. Trouble was, raising taxes to finance spending was very orthodox and represented exactly the kind of old-fashioned thinking that drove the Keynesians wild with despair.

So the economists mobilized, too, arguing that with the economy still weak, a spending increase would increase activity without being inflationary and therefore didn't need to be offset by a tax increase. Worse, they complained, a tax increase would snuff out the nascent recovery.

The economists won Kennedy over. And the sun seemed to shine on them. The recovery continued, inflation abated, and unemployment dropped from 6.8 percent to 6.1 percent in 1961.

The *Economic Report of the President* for 1962 fairly crowed with celebration of the new dogma. In the president's letter, Kennedy said: "The Federal budget played its proper role as a powerful instrument for promoting economic recovery . . . major increases in expenditures for national security and space programs became necessary. In a fully employed economy, these increases would have required new tax revenues to match. But I did not recommend tax increases at this point because they would have cut into private purchasing power and retarded the recovery."

The Council's part of the *Report* is more enthusiastic and smug. Although the economists admitted that the recession probably would have ended early in 1961 in any case, they gave credit to increased government spending for "the impressive pace of the economic expansion." The economists also patted themselves heartily on the back for resisting new taxes to cover spending for the Berlin Wall crisis. And they offered a rather breathless finale for Keynesian achievement: "Finally businessmen and consumers no longer regard prolonged and deep recession as a serious possibility. They generally expect recessions to end quickly; they anticipate a long-term upward trend in the economy; and they spend and invest accordingly. This stability of expectations is in part the result of stability achieved in fact, and reflects general understanding of the structural changes that have contributed to it. But expectations of stability are also the cause of stability—nothing succeeds like success." (Undoubtedly, the Council was a bit premature in its claim. But events in 1962 and on into 1963 seemed to justify this bit of hubris.)

During May 1962, the economists turned up the volume. By June, they felt that Kennedy had been won over. Indeed, the speech he gave at Yale that month constituted a kind of coronation of Keynesian economics. In that speech, Kennedy addressed what he called three major myths. First, that government was big and bad and getting bigger and badder. Second, that budget deficits create inflation. And, third, that corporate plans are based on a political confidence in party leaders; rather, said Kennedy, business confidence is based on a partnership with government to seek "an economic confidence in the nation's ability to invest and produce and consume."

In other words: Sit back and relax, the government has itself under control, it has the budget under control, and it has the country's economy under control. Through fine tuning, flexibility, and turning policy around on a dime, we are stabilizing things. Trust us.

At any rate, while the economists did pull Kennedy on board, Kennedy was never able to pull business along with him. Quite the contrary, business distrusted both Kennedy and the economists—if not the New Economics.

Some of the animosity belongs in the vague category of attitude: Kennedy and his economists had a bad attitude toward business, and businesspeople reciprocated. Kennedy had never been a businessman, had never been in the private sector. His friends were lawyers. His advisers were intellectuals. He had a certain fondness for glitz and glamour, for movie stars and darker characters, not for bankers and widget manufacturers. This blind spot translated as well into his administration. Whereas a third of Eisenhower's top appointments were from business, Kennedy's recruitment efforts focused almost exclusively on those outside the business community.

Nor did the Council go out of its way to communicate with or understand businesspeople. The economists didn't even feel that business was worth asking an opinion of from time to time. As Barbara Bergmann remembers, "We had no real contact with businesspeople and the Council never thought to solicit it."

These slights were not lost on businesspeople, most of whom were Republicans, anyway. Many distrusted academic economists. They felt economists did not understand the risks, responsibilities, and uncertainties of business and, worse, were filled with notions, like fine-tuning the economy, that would add to their stresses and uncertainties.

In general, then, business was concerned about the administration's domestic economic policies, which, they thought, were increasing the size of the government at the expense of the private sector; running budget deficits and adding dangerously to the national debt; requiring the growth of federal spending and encouraging inflation. They also fretted about the administration's interference with their ability to make profits and, more importantly, with the free-enterprise system itself.

A second class of business concern had to do with the weakness of the dollar and the balance of payments deficit. Businesspeople felt that the unfavorable balance of payments was a symptom of irresponsible fiscal and monetary policy—as demonstrated in the outflow of short-term capital.

The dollar, which had been the currency of choice after World War II, began weakening during the mid-1950s. As the rest of the world, especially Europe, prospered, people began off-loading their surplus dollars. This meant cashing in their dollars for gold, then fixed at $35 per ounce. (This, in turn, caused some alarm about a gold drain and gave rise to scary stories that there was no more gold in Fort Knox.) As the U.S. balance of payments worsened, investors, fearing a devaluation of the dollar, started selling, further weakening the dollar. Their reasoning was: If the dollar price of gold was going to be moved up (devaluation), then better to dump, or exchange, your dollars now, before the devaluation.

For all these reasons—from attitudes to actions—the Kennedy administration had a terrible relationship with business. (Although this did not concern his economists, Kennedy was unsettled by it. Heller later told interviewers, "I believe we fairly well persuaded him in 1962 that business confidence would come with high levels of demand and profits. For quite a while, this business confidence issue bothered him, but then he stopped talking about it.")

The failure to get support from the business community put a limit on how far the economists could go in implementing their ideas. Most of their program had not been passed as of November 22, 1963, when Kennedy was assassinated. The economists, simply put, could not put the country's money where their mouths were.

It is fair to say, however, that by the time of Johnson's ascendancy, Keynesianism could no longer be dismissed. The economists had their mouths pressed against the ears of those who had their fingers on the policy levers. Indeed, it looked like the economists had scored several major victories under the Kennedy administration. The economy finished 1962 in excellent shape. Growth logged in at over 5 percent. Unemployment was down and inflation was steady and low. A recession, if one had threatened, had vanished.

Their luck multiplied. The Keynesians had a better, much better, champion in the next president, Lyndon B. Johnson. And the delusion that economic policy could direct the economy reliably, providing good things like growth, employment, and income redistribution and avoiding bad things like inflation, got a full-court workout.

Since part of the Kennedy administration's ineffectiveness was due to its bad relationship with and worse attitude toward the business community, Johnson moved to remedy that. According to Henry Fowler, Johnson's secretary of the treasury (and treasury under secretary for Kennedy), Johnson didn't waste a minute in consolidating business support. "After Dallas, one of Johnson's first acts was to have 45 members of the Business Council and their wives over to the White House for dinner," says Fowler. "He cultivated business the way you would cultivate a garden. What a salesman he was!"

Horace Busby, longtime Johnson friend and adviser, remembers a speech Johnson gave in 1964 at the U.S. Chamber of Commerce annual meeting. "I was surprised that he accepted the invitation, but he obviously wanted to talk to business. He gave a rambling speech before a big crowd, the gist of which was: 'Give me a chance; don't take it out on me.'"

As for the business community, after three years of being on the outs, it was ready to be cultivated. When Johnson opened his arms to business, business pressed against his chest. Leaders stumbled over each other to praise Johnson in the press. He was lauded for his keen insight into private enterprise, his understanding of the need for business to make a profit, and his eschewal of federal spending.

Since, as businesspeople were to discover, Johnson outdid Kennedy in several areas that were anathema to them, the primary source of business attraction to Johnson was a matter of style. Admirers called him charming, detractors called him slick as snake oil, but almost all observers recall that Johnson's personality was hard to resist. (Sure, part of it was the magic of the Oval Office, but a great part of it was, apparently, much back-patting and more than a few dirty jokes.)

Says Alexander Trowbridge, Johnson's secretary of commerce, "I know from watching these Business Council types come to the White House that Johnson would absolutely charm the pants off them. They loved him and went away saying, 'Gee, here's a guy who will really get things done.'"

Johnson, unlike Kennedy, had experience as a businessperson; he appreciated businesspeople, what they did, the power they had, their pragmatism. And all that came through. Johnson was also smarter, quicker, and more interested in economics than Kennedy. But that didn't mean he liked economists. Merton Peck, a member of Johnson's Council, says that Johnson called them " 'the professors'—not in the honorific sense, but more to badger us." Peck goes on, "We regarded our constituency as academic economists, which gave us the pretense or arrogance to represent the public interest. Our neutrality was part of our appeal for Johnson; also, he could disregard our advice at no political cost."

Johnson's indifference to academic advice served him well with the business community but irritated the economists. Instead of having a powerful voice in the administration, as they did with Kennedy, the economists were now just one voice of many. Johnson reached out wide and often for advice. He was constantly on the phone to business leaders. And he didn't hesitate to use their complaints against his own staff. Johnson carried bunches of letters from businesspeople with him. He frequently pulled them out and read them to his economists.

This warm purring toward business was echoed in Johnson's economic reports. While Kennedy's letters introducing the reports were intellectual and even a bit frosty, Johnson's letters were one big wet kiss. While Kennedy's letters gave total credit for economic events to something Olympian and omnipotent called economic policy, Johnson's parceled out credit all around. While Kennedy was all economics, Johnson was all politics.

Of course, it also helped Johnson's case that the economy continued to boom. By the end of 1964, the economy was growing at 5.6 percent annual rate and unemployment had dropped to 5.5 percent. This boom was thought to be the result not just of enlightened economic policy but also of Johnson's special application of it. A *Time* magazine cover story in December 1965, headlined "U.S. Business in 1965," stated: "First the U.S. economists embraced Keynesianism, then the public accepted its tenets. Now even businessmen, traditionally hostile to Government's role in the economy, have been won over—not only because Keynesianism works but because Lyndon Johnson knows how to make it palatable." *Time* went on to describe the rapture: "Businessmen, for their part, have come to accept that the Government should actively use its Keynesian tools to produce growth and stability. They believe that whatever happens, the Government will somehow keep the economy strong and rising."

In other words, the delusion that government policy was successfully managing the economy was now shared by all elements.

Both Johnson's letter and the economists' report were also more aggressive in pushing the New Economics forward. Simply put, with everybody inside the house that Keynes built, it was now time to party. Despite the fact that federal spending had been accelerating, and the government financial commitment to the war on poverty was about to begin, Johnson argued for a tax cut.

As for their contribution, the economists provided the theoretical fuel for gunning the engine. They offered one of those nifty what-if charts showing that under the assumption of full employment, the federal budget would have run a surplus from 1958 onward (in fact, the actual budget was in deficit in 1958, 1959, 1961, 1962, and 1963). This chart allowed the economists to then worry that at full employment, tax revenues would rise substantially, creating, in turn, an increasing drag on the economy. The result? Recession. Their answer? Boost demand by more spending programs and fewer taxes. And, what a happy event, the economists could offer just those things—the income tax cut bill of 1964 and $1 billion to be spent on programs to eradicate poverty. The government could not only reward without sacrifice but was able to grow a healthy economy, too.

And thus the argument was made forcefully for the government to manage economic growth. As Johnson's letter both promised and instructed: "I do not say that we can, at one stroke, wipe out recession or legislate the business cycle out of existence. But vigilant, bold and flexible policy can prevent some recessions and nip others in the bud."

In that year, 1964, the Kennedy income tax cut was finally enacted, the war on poverty began, government revenue increased a tad, government spending increased more than a tad, the budget deficit grew a bit bigger. And it appeared as though everything was working. The economy finished the year in great shape. Growth was strong, up 5.6 percent. Unemployment continued to abate, down to 5 percent, and prices rose a mere 1.2 percent.

Indeed, the economic record was all-round great enough to buoy spirits and generate a little hubris: When time for the 1965 *Report* rolled around, the Council and president not only upped their estimate of potential growth in the economy, but pronounced the business cycle dead.

The government policy to which Johnson gave the most credit was the income tax cut. He noted that it was the first time the government slashed taxes for the purpose of speeding economic growth and that it was done while the economy was growing, rather than languishing. "In short," he wrote, "the tax cut was an expression of faith in the American Economy." As for the business cycle, Johnson added a final note of triumph: "I do not believe recessions are inevitable. . . . We can head them off; or greatly moderate their length and force—if we are able to act promptly."

As always, the Council's portion of the *Report* provided the rationalizations for continued government activity in the economy.

For one thing, the chart of potential and actual economic growth showed that at the usual potential growth rate of 3.5 percent, the gap between potential and actual had narrowed over the past four years. But rather than declaring this a victory, the economists upped the ante by reestimating potential economic growth at 4 percent. This opened up a nice big gap again, one that required even greater federal government activity.

By the spring of 1965, the economy was enjoying a huge boom. In May, the past record of peacetime expansion of 50 consecutive months was broken. And in July, the additional expenditures for the war in Vietnam began to kick in—the start of the conceit known as the "guns-and-butter" economy. Nineteen sixty-five was a good year. Although unemployment was down to 4.1 percent by December, the consumer price index was up a mere 1.7 percent. The budget deficit as a share of the economy had improved to less than 1 percent and economic growth logged in at 5.5 percent.

The period 1965–66 is generally agreed upon by most Keynesians as the moment at which both their popularity and confidence in their model of the economy peaked. *Time* magazine was right. Economics and economists were hot. Paul Samuelson recalls that he said to Heller in 1965, " 'Walter, you sound pretty complacent, but now is the season for it because it won't last.' "

It was, in fact, Heller's 1966 book, *New Dimensions of Political Economy,* that best represents the giddy self-confidence and optimism that characterized the New Economics in the mid-sixties. The book is a trove of here's-the-problem, and-here's-the-answer constructions.

Heller put the economic health of the country smack into the hands of economists, writing that "fiscal strategy has to rely less on the automatic stabilizers and more on discretionary action responding to observed and forecast changes in the economy—less on rules and more on men." (And, goodness knows, they were mostly men.) The ability of the New Economics to shape the world is unquestioned. It is a given that government must step in to provide high levels of employment and growth, "that the market mechanism, left alone, cannot deliver." And he sees a brave new world where "the U.S. economy of the future will be, not recession-proof, but at least recession-repellent."

It may sound unsophisticated now, but the Keynesians really thought they had discovered how to manage the economy to produce growth, price stability, and low unemployment. But 1965 was to be the last year of self-congratulation. Bad policy and bad luck began to catch up with the Keynesians. Cracks in the theoretical foundation were beginning to appear. Some even began to suspect that the New Economics might be as flawed as the old.

In 1966, growth was still strong and unemployment below 4 percent, but inflation was up to a 3.5 percent rate and the deficit as a share of the economy grew a bit larger. And by early 1967, it was clear that the economy was slowing.

These anxieties injected a little balance into the 1967 *Economic Report of the President*. The economists declared that since full employment had been reached, the need to stimulate had to be replaced with restraint and gave credit both to the Fed for its tight money and to fiscal action that bumped up taxes here and there and held down nondefense spending. (Although the major restraint really came from a previously scheduled increase in payroll taxes.) The Council wrote, "By the closing months of 1966, it was shown that policy could work both ways; it could restrain the economy, much as it had been able to provide stimulus during the preceding five years."

As usual, the chart showing potential and actual growth of the economy demonstrated confidence in government economic management. But what a surprise. Even with potential output growing at its new, faster rate of 4 percent, the chart showed that the gap between potential and actual growth had closed! Nineteen sixty-six was the year that the economy was perfect. This perfection presented the economists with a new problem—to keep actual output from rising faster than productive capacity; a strange notion, at any rate.

The economists again made the case for the desirability of active fiscal policy, particularly tax policy, because changes in the tax rates, being such a powerful medicine, could only "be administered in small doses, thus making small adjustments possible." They were very proud of this insight into the power of making small adjustments. Indeed, there was no embarrassment about the fact that in each of the last six years, changes in tax law had become quite common. "The very fact that tax rates are less stable than in the past helps to make for a more stable economy. Far from being a source of increasing uncertainty—as is sometimes alleged—the flexible and coordinated use of stabilization policies should enable both business firms and individuals to make their economic decisions in a climate of greater confidence," wrote the Council. That these policy changes in fact created much disruption and uncertainty would be revealed later.

The year 1967 was weird, from the first half of sag to the last half of zoom. By the end of the year, unemployment was down to 3.8 percent and growth was back up to 2.7 percent, but inflation was a real concern, running at over 4 percent yearly, and the budget deficit as a percent of the economy was getting larger.

The *Economic Report* of 1968 reflected the bad news of the past year. Johnson's letter was uncharacteristically grim, but it did demonstrate the beauty of having given credit for the good times to groups in the economy, rather than to policy, and by then blaming those groups—not policy—for bad times. This Johnson did, scolding both business and labor for causing inflationary pressures.

The Council's portion of the report contained some mealy-mouthedness. The economists affirmed the overall correctness of the active management approach, blaming mistakes in policy on inaction or inadequate action rather than on too much or inappropriate action. But then came a major note of humility. Taking note of the mistakes in forecasting that had begun to build, the economists wrote, "The limitations of the economists' ability to predict the future argue for prudence in policy decisions, flexibility in the use of instruments, and continuing efforts to improve the reliability of forecasting techniques."

At any rate, 1968 was another bad year for the Keynesians. Although they had achieved two of their major goals—unemployment touched a 15-year low of 3.6 percent and the rate of economic growth was up over 4 percent—it was at the cost of two major headaches. The budget deficit as a share of the economy ballooned to over 3 percent and inflation shot up at a 4.2 percent yearly rate.

The *Economic Report* for 1969 would be the last huzzah of the liberal Democrats for some time, and the document's language and spirit reflected this. Johnson, who had already announced that he wasn't running again, reverted to graciousness in his letter. Back are allusions to the successful partnership among business, labor, and government. In a chapter reviewing the past eight years of Keynesian policies, the economists declared success. They called attention to the unprecedented length (seven years) of the economic expansion—versus the 30-month average duration of previous expansions. As for that old devil business cycle: "No longer is the performance of the American economy generally interpreted in terms of stages of the business cycle. No longer do we consider periodic recession once every three or four years an inevitable fact of life."

With that triumph established, the economists drew several lessons about policy—most important, that government actions aimed at influencing economic activity generally worked. Errors, on the other hand, "were errors of omission rather than commission."

Johnson's romance with the business community had lasted about two years; it was followed by a wary distance. By the time Johnson took himself out of the game, in 1968, disillusionment was complete. The administration had lost almost all business support.

Active fiscal policy had proved disruptive, creating punishing uncertainty. There were nine major tax changes during 1962 to 1968, including an off-again, on-again investment tax credit. And government had expanded its areas of concern—especially in social policy, which required greater and greater government spending. Business was worried that Johnson was overloading the system with these programs. "Johnson was intent on changing the world overnight and they, as businesspeople, knew he couldn't," says Trowbridge.

In a sense, the change in business's attitude toward the Johnson administration was an early warning, like the canary dying in the mine shaft, that an activist government was beginning to be the author of problems rather than the answer to them. To be sure, fine tuning was creating uncertainty and, quite apart from the issue of whether fine tuning was working, was the concern that the costs of continually switching policies were too high. But if fine tuning wasn't working—as some were beginning to suspect, looking at the performance of the economy—then government fiddling was generating a double burden, uncertainty compounded.

One of Johnson's economists, Arthur Okun, addressed this issue squarely, if disingenuously, in speaking about business wariness over swings in policy. He noted that government activism has focused an unusual amount of attention on Washington in areas in which government decisions were especially important to business—defense spending, taxes, and credit policy—admitting that those areas have become important sources of uncertainty and disruption to business planning. Yet, Okun concluded rather unselfconsciously, "The businessman has good reason to wish that the economic policy planner would retreat into a corner . . . and take his shadow off the business scene." And that wish became even more fervent with the next president. When it came to creating economic uncertainty and disruption, Richard Nixon proved to be a master.

Indeed, the decade of the 1970s was a veritable fiesta of Keynesian management. As the economy slumped—and slumped again—the administrations of Nixon, Ford, and Carter were unable to take their hands off the economic tiller. The Keynesian promise that government policy could direct the economy to provide good and steady growth proved too seductive to abandon. The 1980s represented a brief and rather faint respite—the Reagan administration was less besotted with active government—but things returned to business as usual with the Bush and Clinton administrations.

The amount of pushing and pulling that the economy has been subject to since the Keynesian revolution was embraced by policy makers is made clear by looking at four categories in which the economy has suffered most. It is fair to say that these four areas experienced overheated government management just because they bore the burden of flaws in the Keynesian model. Consider:

Inflation has been a giant trouble because the theory simply discounted its danger and, even after the danger was recognized, could not account for it.

The tax code has been whipsawed because that area of management was taken to be supremo for managing economic growth.

The federal budget deficit is out of control because deficits were the inevitable result of a theory that leaned on government spending and extolled the virtues of running deficits.

And regulation of the economy has become a daily frustration because once the assumption of an all-powerful government was accepted, it was only natural to use such a mighty force to achieve all sorts of goals by allowing it to determine the shape of activity.

The next part of this book takes a closer look at these problem areas.

Part III

How Big,
Busy Government
Affects
the Economy

6

Inflation

Inflation, it is generally agreed, is chiefly the result of the Federal Reserve Bank providing more money to the economy than the economy can absorb and still maintain a stable price level. That is, inflation is what happens when the amount of money circulating exceeds what is necessary for people to make transactions. For example, say the Federal Reserve floods the economy with money. People will continue to buy cars and haircuts, but if the number of cars and haircuts remains constant, or grows more slowly than does the amount of money, the "extra" money will translate into higher prices. And higher prices throughout the economy is just another way of saying that the economy is experiencing inflation. In fact, all this is nothing more than an elaboration of the statement that inflation is caused by too much money chasing too few goods.

The problems with inflation are many. Its main mischief is to create uncertainty. Absent stable prices, people cannot count on the future value of goods and services, making it more difficult for them to plan. This uncertainty undermines long-term contracts; for example, workers are reluctant to make wage agreements if they suspect that the value of their wages will be eroded by inflation, and creditors of any kind are loath to lend money out if they think they will be paid back in money that is worth less because rising prices mean the money will buy less than when they lent it out.

The devastating impact of inflation was made quite clear during the 1970s, when the rate of inflation increased to double digits, pushing up interest rates (and mortgage rates and consumer credit rates) to punishingly high levels. People consumed lots of time and energy trying to protect themselves against inflation. In fact, the virtue of stable prices is now so clear that when the slightest signal of inflation is given by any of the indices that track prices (like the Consumer Price Index or the Producer Price Index), financial markets respond instantly, often due to anxiety rather than to an actual event. The bond market, for example, is particularly sensitive to even a whiff of inflation—long-term creditors pull back, forcing interest rates up.

It wasn't always thus. During the 1960s, many powerful and smart people discounted the danger of inflation. They were foolish, and the debilitating inflation of the 1970s was a direct result.

Inflationary policies grew out of an incorrect theory of what does and does not cause inflation. For Keynesians, inflation was a wage-price phenomenon that occurred when, somehow, the economy became caught up in a price-wage spiral. The formulation ran something like this: Rising living costs support demands for wage increases in excess of productivity gains. The resulting bulge in labor costs shows up in even higher prices. These price and wage increases keep on reinforcing each other long after the initial source of inflation has ceased to operate. Thus, the spiral can continue to turn more or less on its own momentum.

Just how this spiral started—why living costs started to mount—was left vague. The explanation generally attributed this initial impetus to an increase in the money supply that lowered interest rates, which then generated a burst of business and consumer spending, thus pushing up prices. But it is not unfair to say that Keynesians felt inflation was caused when the economy was suddenly zapped by aliens from the Planet Debbie who caused prices to rise, which caused wages to rise, thereby causing prices to rise, thereby causing wages to rise, and so on.

Surely, Keynesians tended to be dismissive of the importance of monetary policy in causing inflation. When monetarists started putting out their ideas in the mid-1960s, Keynesians were hostile. Hendrik Houthakker, a member of the Council during the Johnson administration, showed chief economist Gardner Ackley his paper demonstrating that growth in the nominal economy was a function of money supply a year earlier. "Gardner, normally a sweet man, wasn't even interested. He thought it was crackpot," says Houthakker.

Oddly, this blind spot persisted well into the next decade. In the 1970s, Arthur Okun, a Johnson administration economist, was asked by interviewers about a previous statement on economic ignorance. Okun replied: "We know that none of our inflation theories really explained the behavior of the price level in the last decade. . . . A lot of us individually think that we do have a better clue to what really goes on in the economy and why it is as resistant to . . . cooling off as it is, but there is no accepted new theory of inflation that will do the job."

According to Keynesian theory, the importance of the Federal Reserve lay in its role of supplying enough money to keep interest rates low and economic activity humming. Since they blamed inflation on a wage-price spiral, they weren't worried about the Fed supplying too much money and thereby driving up the price level; indeed, Keynesians thought that inflation could be kept in the bag if government held down wages and prices in the private sector. Also, it was a Keynesian article of faith that fear of inflation was misplaced, perhaps even a touch hysterical, because they thought that tolerating a little inflation could bring a lot more employment.

In practice, this meant that Keynesians were always hectoring the Fed to be a little looser in providing money to the economy and hectoring business and workers to hold down prices and wages. In other words, at the same time they were encouraging inflation with a loose monetary policy, they were trying to limit its impact by forbidding management and labor to cope.

A look at the course of inflation and policies to combat it during the 1960s and 1970s shows just how futile these wage-price policies were.

The Kennedy administration's main weapon against inflation was something called wage-and-price guideposts, which were trotted out in the 1962 *Economic Report;* they called on workers and business to restrict wage and price changes to changes in productivity. The argument was that Keynesian policies would generate a full-employment, high-growth economy that might cause inflation; thus, wage-price restraints were necessary. The guideposts were also a kind of fallback position to improve the Phillips curve trade-off of so much employment for so much inflation. They were a fine-tuning device aimed at permitting the economy to achieve lower unemployment without much inflation.

The whole thing was a rather silly exercise. The guidelines were not binding, so there was little cost in ignoring them, and, in any case, neither labor nor management liked the government breathing over its shoulder in wage or price decisions.

The first big test of Keynesian anti-inflation strategy came with the so-called steel crisis. In early 1961, with an economic recovery clearly visible, the coming talks between the union and steelmakers loomed large. The economists wanted to avoid a big wage increase and the price increase that was sure to follow, so the administration jawboned both sides.

Big steel did, in fact, forgo a price increase in the fall of 1961, but most executives resented Kennedy's interference, based, as it was, on the Council's inadequate understanding of the industry. An understanding that, according to Barbara Bergmann, then a Council staff member, was gleaned from reading *Popular Mechanics*. "We lectured them on whether they had made the correct investment decisions and told them they would lose market share," she says. Roger Blough, head of U.S. Steel, took umbrage at Kennedy's suggestion that steel prices should not be raised based on profit forecasts provided by the Council. "The President's attempt to predetermine the prices of the steel industry was, to my knowledge, an unprecedented move in the history of our country at peacetime," he wrote later in *Life* magazine.

In January 1962, both sides agreed to start meeting on a new contract four months ahead of the expiration date. The talks broke down, were restarted, and so forth—with Kennedy continuing to play governess. Thus, the administration was thrilled when the new contract, announced in March, was quite reasonable and modest. It was taken as a triumph for the administration's hands-on strategy.

But all the more reason for the administration to go berserk when, in April, U.S. Steel announced that it was raising prices by 3.5 percent in order to catch up with cost pressures that had been building for four years. (This move prompted Kennedy's famous comment: "My father told me that all businessmen were sons of bitches, but I never believed it until now.") The next day, seven other major producers announced price increases. It is fair to say that the administration felt humiliated. And it had a massive hissy fit.

Five companies did not raise prices. Immediately, the Council pushed a divide-and-conquer strategy. Walter Heller said later to interviewers: "I knew some people at Armco, others knew people at Inland Steel and Kaiser, and when those three promised to hold out, there was just no way that U.S. Steel could hold its price . . . we took the little ones and picked them off one by one, and we are inclined to think that in that sense economics broke the price increase." But success did not wholly belong to the economists—the administration also intimidated producers by making free use of midnight visits from the FBI, antitrust subpoenas, grand jury investigations, congressional hearings, withholding Pentagon contracts, and threats of hostile legislation.

Seventy-two hours later, Bethlehem Steel rescinded its increase after the Pentagon awarded a $5 million contract to a company that had not raised prices. Then U.S. Steel gave in. The crisis was over.

The steel industry settlement was probably within the guideposts, but other 1962 settlements in the railroad, airline, and construction industries were a touch over the limit. As were pay raises for federal employees—averaging more than a whopping 6 percent. The following year, several other settlements violated the guideposts (including, again, that for government employees).

During the Johnson administration, a booming economy made the guideposts even more nettlesome. Labor was enjoying high employment, which gave them the bargaining clout to get big wage increases. Too, as inflation raised the cost of living, workers became even more reluctant to accept a wage ceiling—which was put at 3.2 percent. And business felt less constrained about raising prices to absorb such costs.

In 1964, a bunch of settlements violated the guidelines. A major contract between the auto industry and the UAW permitted increases of over 4 percent, and settlements in the cement, glass, and container industries were also over the 3.2 percent limit. And, again, wage increases for federal employees were excessive. No surprise that in 1964, wage increases exceeded growth in productivity.

As inflation picked up steam in the fall of 1965, the Johnson administration got tough, hoping to log at least one important settlement within the guideposts. How tough? Plenty. The administration threatened to dump over 1.4 million tons of aluminum from its stockpile, thereby driving down prices, if the aluminum industry did not take back a price hike. Ditto for the copper industry. Further, a threat to shift defense contracts to producers who didn't raise prices was used successfully in negotiations with the steel industry. (Again, that year, a major violator of the guideposts was the government—federal civilian and military pay increases were in excess of the guideposts.)

In 1966, the Council held negotiations with dozens of producers, threatening to use the government powers in purchasing, stockpile sales, and foreign trade regulations (e.g., rescinding import duties or imposing export controls) to hammer down prices. There were confrontations in the lumber, textile, molybdenum, and sulfur industries and pointed stockpile sales of tungsten, vanadium, and rubber.

However, it was clear that the wage-price program was in trouble when inflation took a big bump-up to over 3 percent. The end came with the settlement of the airline machinists' strike. The union had already rejected an arbitration board's recommendation of a 3.5 percent increase when Johnson endorsed one at 4.3 percent, even though it was in utter violation of the guideposts. The union rejected that offer, finally accepting a 4.9 percent increase. And the administration rolled over. Its surrender made any further defense of the guideposts impossible. After that, there were several new contracts with wage increases around the 5 percent mark.

In 1967, major union settlements provided wage and benefit increases averaging about 5.5 percent a year over the life of the contract, while average hourly compensation in the entire private economy rose by 6 percent.

Meanwhile, what was happening back at the ranch? Although signs of inflation had grown more numerous in 1965, there was little action on the monetary front. After several years of a very loose policy, the Fed did begin to tighten up on the supply of money in December 1965. Interest rates started to creep up—from 4 percent in December 1965 to 5.75 percent by August 1966. And by September, the Fed's policies seemed to have reached the alarmingly effective stage, particularly by decking the housing industry. A financial crisis was feared. At this point, the Fed shifted to a less restrictive policy. Simply put, the Fed reversed its course, loosening at the first hint of economic distress.

After the Republican victory in 1968, the Johnson administration more or less gave up on managing wage-price decisions. In 1969, the last *Economic Report* of the Kennedy-Johnson years blames the "blemished record" of the guideposts on an overheated economy and the fact that neither labor nor business was involved in developing them, thus cutting off the possibility of cooperation.

On its face, this is true. Neither business nor labor was consulted and the guideposts were intrusive in any case. There was no emergency situation to justify an intrusion into what were after all decisions made by consenting adults. Quite the contrary; since inflation was creeping up all around them, those consenting adults felt justified in pushing up wages and prices. But, at a deeper level, the guideposts didn't work because the Fed's loose monetary policy was underwriting the speedup of inflation.

And although the guideposts were not successful in keeping wages (and some prices) from going up faster than productivity growth, they were successful in distorting decisions and market allocations. Because some prices were kept artificially low—particularly where rollbacks were obtained in basic industries—false signals were sent to consumers of those products, thereby keeping demand unrealistically high. Furthermore, by not allowing prices to keep pace with rising costs, the guideposts limited business's ability to expand production—thereby creating inflationary shortages. In short, the guideposts created a mess without preventing inflation.

And inflation there was. Most notably, when the Fed eased money growth in 1967, it fired up the rate of inflation to 5 percent.

Thus, inflation, which wasn't supposed to happen under government activism, had indeed happened. The wage-price guideposts, which were not supposed to be mandates, took on an ominous edge when accompanied by the government's manipulating of the market with stockpile selling, and threats, like redirecting defense contracts. But rather than rethinking the problem, the Keynesians just hardened their view. The wage-price guidelines were a soft-focus dress rehearsal when compared with what followed—wage-price controls in the early 1970s.

When Nixon became president in 1969, his administration tried to cool inflation with a bunch of standard maneuvers. The new fiddle in the policy mix was an emphasis on monetary policy. As discussed, the Keynesian approach to inflation was inadequate from beginning to end. They didn't understand what caused it, so their solutions were powerless to stop it.

There was, however, a person—and a theoretical school—that understood very well where inflation came from and had a simple solution to stop it. Meet Milton Friedman and the monetarists.

Friedman, and what was known as the Chicago School, had been grousing about inflation for almost a decade. They argued that inflation was caused by the Fed pumping too much money into the economy; that is, when the growth in the money supply exceeded the rate of growth in the economy, the result was inflation. Further, Friedman didn't hold with the received wisdom that high inflation causes high growth and low unemployment and vice versa. His point was that only unexpected inflation could bring down unemployment—and then only temporarily—because wages would go up more slowly than prices in such an environment and thus make labor relatively cheap for a time.

Moreover—and here's what really annoyed the Keynesians—monetarists said that booms or busts were caused by changes in the money supply, not by fiscal policy. In this view, too much money in the economy leads to a boom in the short term and an increase in the general price level (inflation) in the long term; too little money leads to busts in the short term and decreases in prices in the long term (deflation); and up-and-down changes in the money supply leads to an up-and-down economy. Hence, monetary policy was more important than fiscal policy.

Not that fiscal policy was impotent; Friedman felt that fiscal policy could cause great harm, particularly one that stimulated the economy through budget deficits if the Fed printed money to accommodate the increase in federal borrowing.

The Nixon administration tried to play the fight against inflation both ways by paying lip service to monetarists and fiscalists. In its 1970 *Report,* the economists argued that inflation had been caused by three events: mounting budget deficits, rapid monetary expansion that began in 1965 with the escalation of the Vietnam War, and massive increases in federal spending for domestic programs.

The Council noted that there were disagreements among economists about the relative roles of these events and that these differences led to different policies. One was that the budget should run a moderate surplus; the other was that there should be a decisive reduction of the rate of monetary growth. The administration decided that it couldn't choose one to the exclusion of the other, so it chose both.

At any rate, the monetary part of the dispute was settled when the Fed finally clamped down on money creation. Tightness in monetary policy during 1969 was severe. The growth rate in the money supply fell from 8 percent in 1968 to under 3 percent in 1969; meanwhile, interest rates shot up, from 5.6 percent in 1968 to 7.3 percent in 1969.

Monetarists complained that the Fed was too tight and that a recession would result. This was the substance of a cover story in *Time* in December 1969, slugged "The Rising Risk of Recession." *Time* described a recession anxiety that "has been intensified by the bearish warnings of one economist who was once ignored and ridiculed, but whose views have lately had an important influence on Government policy. He is Milton Friedman, the leading iconoclast of U.S. economics. 'We are heading for a recession at least as sharp as that in 1960–61,' he warns." The article ended by reporting that Friedman believed that the United States would go through an "inflationary recession"—increases in both prices and unemployment.

He was right. And the economy got a tiny taste of the stagflation that began in earnest in 1974. Tight monetary policy in 1969 became, with the predicted lag, a recession in 1970. Unemployment rose to 6 percent and the growth rate was zero. The administration was charged with overkill. But the worst part was that wages and prices continued to rise. The recession had no impact on inflation.

Why? Because, after five years of climbing inflation rates, people expected that inflation was a permanent part of the economic landscape and behaved accordingly. There were even newspaper contests to update clichés for inflation. Hence, cats were said to have 10 lives, it took three to tango, and four was a crowd. Expectations of inflation had become embedded.

Pressure for more decisive government action increased. In August 1970, Congress passed the Economic Stabilization Act, giving Nixon authority to freeze wages, salaries, prices, and rents. Nobody really expected that Nixon would exercise this authority—indeed, he insisted he would not use it.

By the end of 1970, the inflation rate had hit 5.5 percent and increases in average major wage settlements were up to almost 9 percent as workers tried to limit the damage from inflation over the life of their labor contracts.

Inflation kept steaming right along in the beginning of 1971. The level of wage settlements increased, while unemployment hovered at 6 percent. In January 1971, when Nixon submitted his budget, he proudly announced, "Now I am a Keynesian." The budget was expansionary, to stimulate economy, but would not be in deficit at full employment. That is, the budget would balance if employment were "full" and, in spending as if the economy were at full employment, full employment would be attained. This was, of course, a terrible mishmash of Keynesian rationalizations for the government to spend more than it took in to stimulate the economy, while achieving the conservative goal of balancing the budget.

Nixon was firm about wage-price controls: "Free prices and wages are the heart of our economic system; we should not stop them from working even to cure an inflationary fever. I do not intend to impose wage and price controls which would substitute new, growing and more vexatious problems for the problems of inflation." Just months later came Nixon's New Economic Policy with wage-price controls.

Pressure for wage-price intervention had been growing; it came from both Democrats and Republicans, from businesspeople, trade groups, and editorial columnists. Public opinion polls showed huge popular support. The coming election of 1972 also contributed to the pressure since it would be difficult for both parties to run on a record of reducing inflation by a tad but increasing unemployment a lot. "The Nixon administration didn't want to get stuck with a weak recovery and strong inflation, and given the developing situation, you looked pigheaded if you didn't do anything," says Marvin Kosters, an administration economist. "The stock market and public opinion were very much in favor of a freeze."

As great as the domestic incentives were, however, it was finally the weakness of the dollar that forced the administration to act. The dollar had been overvalued for more than a decade. Back then, of course, the United States was on the version of the gold standard established in 1944. One ounce of gold was worth $34 and other major currencies were fixed at a par value to the dollar. An overvalued dollar meant that there were more dollars out in the world than the world needed to buy things from the United States. That is, the world was selling more to the United States (so we were spending more abroad) than it was buying from the United States (so we were earning less from exports) as evidenced by a persistent deficit in the balance of payments.

As a result, foreign governments were accumulating more and more dollars. Under the gold standard, the United States had an obligation to buy back those dollars with gold, offering one ounce for $34. This meant that other nations could say, "Aha! Since the dollar is overvalued, we can buy one ounce of gold for $34, even though gold is worth $40." This was a good deal for them but meant a gold drain for the United States.

The administration had several choices—two unpleasant and one (theoretically, at least) somewhat desirable. The two toughies would be to either devalue the dollar—accept reality and declare that it now took $40 to buy one ounce of gold—or to straighten out domestic policies to strengthen the dollar back to the point where one ounce of gold was actually worth $34. The seductive choice would be to just wash the nation's hands of the gold standard and change to a floating exchange rate system. Not that the problems in ending the gold standard weren't known: The dollar would depreciate, which, in turn, would raise the price of imports and add to inflation; ending the gold standard could also be read as a sign that, by cutting its last link to price stability, the United States had given up the battle against inflation.

On August 15, 1971, Nixon suspended the convertibility of the dollar into gold. This single act is blamed by many economists for the rampant inflation during the rest of the decade. He tried to offset inflationary pressure from the end of the gold standard by announcing the first peacetime controls on wages and prices in the nation's history with a freeze that was to begin immediately and last until November.

Both the end of the gold standard and a wage-price freeze were very serious measures—the end of the gold standard because the world had been functioning on it for the past 30 years and Nixon's action was unilateral; and the freeze because it constituted heavy government interference in the economy.

A freeze meant a freeze. Paul McCracken said later to interviewers: "I remember a little trucker who had concluded a contract with his drivers. His sole customer was A&P. A&P had agreed once he concluded his labor contract, they would estimate rates appropriate to the higher costs. The freeze came right in the middle. He claimed that he probably would go bankrupt if he didn't get some immediate relief. I don't remember all the details, but the IRS audited his books and corroborated the fact that he'd probably go broke. We still ruled against him. I don't know whether he went broke or not."

Less dire but just as typical was the great jelly bean dispute recalled by Marvin Kosters. Halloween came during the freeze, and jelly bean manufacturers wanted permission to raise the price on orange and black jelly beans. They argued variously that the price increase be granted under the "new products" rule and/or the "seasonality" rule. They were overruled. "It is true that we were quite arbitrary and grossly unfair," says Kosters, looking back on those days. "It was really quite horrible when we had to apply the rules to individual cases; the injustice of the freeze was really jarring."

At any rate, the program, named the New Economic Policy, lasted from 1971 to 1974. It's hard to bill it as a strictly Republican program, since the Democrats controlled Congress during its four phases. Generally speaking, the New Economic Policy coupled wage-price controls with very stimulative fiscal and monetary policies to reduce unemployment. It looked like it was working, briefly, but its net effect was a raging inflation and high unemployment together.

The freeze did not cut the inflation rate to zero, but it did come down to less than 2 percent during its three-month tenure. Of course, that result is inevitable: if prices are capped, then rising prices can't rise but falling ones will fall, so the price index will head down. Whether the freeze cured inflation, however, is another question entirely. As McCracken later told interviewers, "I would say no, it did not."

The second phase, which lasted from November 1971 to January 1973, was a mandatory program allowing prices and wages to move up, but not too far. Wages were held to a 5.5 percent increase and prices could go up according to a complicated formula. Both wage and price increases moderated through 1972. Phase III called for voluntary compliance with general wage and price standards. The administration thought that inflation could be held to 3 percent for 1973, with unemployment down around 4 percent. Oh, boy, were they wrong.

To be fair, the international markets didn't give their forecast a true test. Two mega-problems took the economy by storm. By late 1972, worldwide crop failures, including those in the Soviet Union, were putting pressure on the U.S. food supply, particularly grain and soybeans. In 1973, farm and food prices skyrocketed: prices for wheat, corn, and chickens more than doubled. Meanwhile, the dollar was sinking. It had been devalued in December 1971, but international confidence continued to erode, leading to another devaluation in February 1973. The dollar kept falling on the exchange markets, pushing up import prices and feeding inflation. By the end of Phase III, inflation was worse, running at an annual rate of 10 percent.

The administration then reversed itself, announcing a 60-day freeze in June 1973. It was a total flop and was lifted in July when Phase IV began, a return to mandatory controls. But by this time it was clear that the controls were not working and that inflation was resurgent. Phase IV had almost zero impact and was allowed to die quietly in April 1974.

Overall, it's hard to say that the wage-price controls worked. Prices increased at an almost 7 percent annual rate over the 1971–74 period. Whether they would have gone up faster, of course, would have depended on how tight money was absent controls. What controls did do, however, was distort price signals coming from the market, offer opportunities for evasion, and create a large enforcement bureaucracy.

About the time that the controls were allowed to lapse, the economy was hit by a second shock—this one from the Organization of Petroleum Exporting Countries (OPEC). In October 1973, OPEC began cutting production and its members embargoed oil to the United States. By March of the next year, when the embargo ended, the price of oil had quadrupled. Although most of the impetus for the embargo was U.S. support for Israel during the Arab-Israeli war, OPEC was also driven by the fact that the value of oil, which was priced in dollars, had been cheapened by the weak dollar and inflation.

The Federal Reserve responded to the oil shock by flooding the economy with money—popularly thought of as "inflating our way out of difficulty." The idea was that if oil suddenly cost more, then the economy needed more money to buy it. In August 1974, when Nixon resigned, inflation was up again to 12 percent and by the end of the year, wholesale prices were up 18 percent.

The failure of both wage-price guidelines and controls should have alerted policy makers to the fact that there was something deeply wrong with the way they were trying to do business. It didn't. Although no administration has tried to exercise such government control over the economy again, there was very little rethinking of the Keynesian approach during the 1970s. The result, of course, was that inflation got worse.

The next president, Gerald Ford, also labored in vain to stop inflation. Oddly, his chief economist, Alan Greenspan, was not one of those Keynesian sops who discounted the danger from inflation or believed in the Phillips curve trade-off. He thought that since unemployment and inflation went up together, they could be brought down together. Greenspan's prescription for stopping inflation—cut the growth of federal spending, thereby cutting the level of federal financing, thereby bringing down the rate of growth in the money supply—would have had a positive impact. Too bad the rest of the administration didn't listen.

Ford took office, calling inflation "Public Enemy Number 1." His program had a little bit of everything and not much of anything. He also introduced the infamous WIN button—Whip Inflation Now—shorthand for a voluntary program asking Americans to fight inflation by saving more, working harder, conserving energy, and behaving with greater charity toward the less fortunate. During its four-month existence, the WIN button became the emblem of muddleheaded policy, its mere display caused people to chuckle. The Ford administration ended its tenure with inflation at 9 percent.

But the worst record on inflation was yet to come. It belongs to the Carter administration. In spring of 1978, with inflation accelerating, President Jimmy Carter announced a new anti-inflation program of wage and price guidelines. They worked about as well as they had under Kennedy, and inflation ended the year running at an almost 8 percent rate.

In his letter for the 1979 *Economic Report,* Carter blamed inflation on almost everything under the sun except the loose monetary policy that was, in fact, driving it. He ascribed the higher rate to a cold winter, which reduced food supplies and ballooned prices; the depreciation of the dollar, which made imports more expensive and allowed U.S. firms to raise their prices; poor growth in productivity; and the cumulative effects of regulation, which contributed to cost pressures. Carter promised to reduce the budget deficit by slowing the growth in government spending. He also called for monetary restraint by the Fed.

As 1979 unfolded, the inflation rate accelerated. So the administration abandoned its initial policy for one of firmer fiscal restraint. That, along with a second oil shock, brought the threat of a recession. (Between 1978 and 1980, OPEC raised oil prices from $13 to $32 a barrel. Part of the jump was due to the revolution in Iran against the shah, when a strike stopped Iranian exports in 1979. After exports resumed, OPEC eventually settled on $23.50 a barrel.)

Carter's chief economist, Charles Schultze, later told interviewers that the choice was "either run the economy through a major recession—but no president would do that—or we could do what we did, kind of half-ass, some austerity and some jawboning. But it wasn't enough and it didn't work." And how could it? At the same time, the Fed was swamping the economy with money. Growth in the money supply was greater in the three years from 1977 through 1979 than in any other three years during the postwar period. The result was textbook: The inflation rate smoked up to almost 12 percent.

Finally, when the annual rate of inflation pierced 13 percent, the Federal Reserve Board, under chairperson Paul Volcker, began its regime of controlling the money supply to check inflation. The clampdown began in October of 1979; it sent interest rates soaring, as it was supposed to do. But, worse, after interest rates spiked in January, the administration sat on credit with the 1980 Credit Control Act aimed at checking consumer buying. The act was so effective that many observers blamed the steep recession that followed on those controls. In March, a *Time* cover story noted that "Inflation and interest rates both topping 18 percent are so far beyond anything that Americans have experienced in peacetime . . . as to inspire a contagion of fear." For once, *Time* could not be accused of hyperbole.

After a brief (but wicked) recession, inflation continued to fall while the economy and employment grew. That fact demonstrated not only that the Phillips curve trade-off was wrong, but also settled the question, once and for all, about the importance of monetary policy: When the Federal Reserve decisively and determinedly cracked down on money creation, it broke the back of inflation. While monetarists may have lost some credibility later in the decade by making wildly erroneous forecasts, nobody now doubts the connection between profligate money creation and inflation.

Although it was Volcker's regime of tight money that brought relief, credit must also go to the next president, Ronald Reagan, who supported Volcker. In the Reagan administration's first *Economic Report,* inflation was classified as essentially a monetary phenomenon and therefore under the control of the Federal Reserve Board. While the Fed's tight monetary policy was fingered as the primary cause of the recession, no blame was attached. The administration admitted that the short-term costs were sharp and unfortunate, but that the benefits—lower rates of inflation—were worth the pain. Indeed, it admonished that any weakening in resolve would blow the Fed's credibility and fire up inflationary expectations, making the pain more acute.

As for any good coming from inflation, like lower unemployment, the Reagan economists had only to present the actual experience of the Phillips curve. Page 51 of the 1982 *Report* has a hilarious chart showing two decades of the Phillips curve. From 1961 to 1969, it does look as if there were a trade-off, with unemployment coming down and inflation going up; from 1970 to 1981, however, the line describing the trade-off goes nuts, tracing circles of both high inflation and high unemployment.

With a monetarist regime thus set and a tight monetary policy in place, the rate of inflation decelerated—actually dropped—from 12.5 percent in 1980 through 1983, when it hit 3.8 percent. It remained in the 3 to 4 percent range until 1988, when it rose briefly, hitting 6 percent in 1990. After that, more relief, with an annual rate of under 3 percent from 1992 to 1994. Indeed, after 1982, the rate of inflation was so well behaved that it ceased to be a front-page issue.

Until 1994, that is. That's when the Federal Reserve, responding to scattered inflation signals, began to inch up short-term interest rates every several months. When rates got high enough to slow the economy, almost everybody started yelping about the Fed taking away the punch bowl just as the party got started.

Surely there is a better way.

Start with the indisputable notion that price stability—no inflation—is good. A zero rate of inflation would restore the ability to plan for the long term. Businesspeople and investors could borrow without anxiety and hedging, and invest with confidence that payoffs from projects can be known; lenders would be more sanguine about providing credit, thereby supplying more credit and lowering interest rates. Moreover, with zero inflation, price signals coming from the market would be clearer and more easily understood.

Achieving zero inflation would not be difficult. One way would be to reinstate the gold, or a commodity, standard. But that is probably not politically doable. Another, much more achievable, way would involve a tiny and intelligent change in the Humphrey-Hawkins Act of 1978. As it stands, the act requires the Federal Reserve to do two things—maintain a stable price level and a full employment rate. But the Fed can only affect prices, it cannot produce more jobs (no matter how inflationary its policy); thus, the jobs requirement should be dropped. This would free the Fed to do what it can, in fact, do: set a timetable to reach zero inflation and then follow it until the goal is reached by keeping the growth rate of the money supply pegged to growth in the real economy.

Pretty simple stuff.

Three decades of stop-and-go monetary policy and volatile inflation and interest rates are quite enough. A stable price level would give the economy an excellent chance to prosper—and it would give those silly metaphors about the Fed taking away the punch bowl just when the party gets started a rest.

7

Taxes

There are many ways in which policies can infuriate and frus-
trate, but taxation belongs in a special category. We seem to
be intensely sensitive to giving our money to the government—this
is, after all, a nation that got its start by rejecting taxes levied by its
mom, the British government. Yet unlike some economic ills—inflation, budget deficits, regulation—taxes are necessary. It's how
government gets the money needed to perform the tasks we require of it.

But beyond the obviously unpleasant aspect of giving the
government this money is the fact that taxes can give rise to inefficient behavior or activity. Levying a tax on something increases its
relative price, which distorts price signals coming from the market;
that, in turn, alters economic behavior. Consider: When a product
is taxed, it creates an incentive for people to purchase less of it.
When an activity is taxed, it creates an incentive for people to shift

into other, less taxed activities. For example, if wages bear a large tax, especially at the margin where the last dollar earned is taxed at a higher rate than the rest of the dollars, it creates an incentive for people not to work for that last dollar but to substitute leisure activity, which is not taxed. If certain investments or returns on them are highly taxed, then investors might favor projects in which the returns are less taxed or that confer a tax advantage by generating deductible losses.

In some cases, behavior can be so altered that the good or service that bears the levy can be "taxed out of business." A tax on bananas, for example, means that bananas cost more money. All other things being equal, people will buy fewer taxed bananas than they did untaxed ones. A really stiff tax on the fruit could put growers on unemployment.

But just as other ploys to alter behavior can have unintended consequences, so can tax policy. For example, the incentive impact can pop up in the wrong way: that's just what happened with the 1990 luxury tax when rich people eluded their intended soaking, which then left the middle class to get wet. Or taxes might create opposing incentives, with the desired one overwhelmed by the undesirable: Lower marginal taxes on earned income may not result in more work effort if lower taxes give people sufficiently more disposable income and hence less incentive to work.

Or tax policy may fail to achieve its objective in other ways. At any one time in an economic system as complicated as ours, some policies are canceled out by other policies or stronger forces. Not even the most exquisitely designed tax policy can overcome otherwise miserable growth conditions produced by things like war or pestilence.

Nonetheless, because taxes can be so powerful in changing behavior, the main purpose of taxation—to raise revenue—is often ignored in favor of other purposes. Thus, tax policy is a favorite tool of government to reward certain groups and punish others, or to encourage one activity over another. Indeed, it is this power that makes taxation attractive to policy makers as a tool for "managing" economic growth. One familiar formulation runs: If the economy is sluggish, a tax cut will put more money into the hands of consumers and businesspeople who, presumably, will spend it, thereby stimulating growth; if the economy is racing, then a tax increase can be enacted to take money away from consumers and businesspeople who, presumably, will spend less, thereby slowing growth.

The notion of using taxation for economic management was first seriously introduced and employed by the Keynesians in the 1960s. Their emphasis was on cutting taxes to increase the spending power of consumers and business. (They were not bothered by the fact that government would have less revenue to spend; government could maintain or increase spending by running a budget deficit.)

The result was an extravaganza of tax manipulation for the purpose of directing economic growth. Unfortunately, the net effect of constant tinkering was not what was anticipated in the short run. And in the long run, the tax system became a maze of distortions and perverse incentives so that resources, which would otherwise be valued at their use to society and allowed to earn their highest return, were evaluated for their tax consequences and earned suboptimal returns for society.

From the moment the Keynesians arrived in Washington, they began to nag President Kennedy to cut income taxes as part of their high-growth agenda. Kennedy resisted. Politically, he thought it was unwise, since he had been elected on a program of sacrifice. From an economic point of view, he argued that cutting taxes was not necessary, given that the economy was growing and the federal budget ought to be balanced.

The economists responded that the economy could be even stronger, and tax cuts were the proper way to stimulate it. They were not at all worried about a tax cut causing a budget deficit. Rather, they felt that their goals of faster growth and higher employment could be achieved by fewer taxes and a bigger budget deficit, both of which would spur spending.

The fight for the minds of the president and the public over this issue was rather interestingly described by Kennedy's chief economist, Walter Heller, in an interview years later. Heller figured that they had convinced Kennedy by the end of 1961, "getting him fairly well educated on modern economics." When Kennedy pledged to propose a tax cut in 1963, it was, according to Heller, "the first real major commitment of a U.S. President to a truly modern fiscal policy involving tax cuts in the face of deficit financing, a rising budget and a rising economy. That was simply unprecedented."

About the rest of the country, Heller said: "We had to sell modern fiscal policy to an unbelieving and highly suspicious public. One way to sell it—and this, I guess, was a fringe benefit of going the tax route—was to get business on board to help sell modern economics through a tax cut, which was dear to the hearts of business. They'd always previously said, 'You can't have a tax cut until you've got a surplus in the budget.' Here we sold them deficit financing through a tax cut, and they in turn helped to sell it to the country."

It's not clear that business really signed off on the tax cuts. At least not immediately. But the 1964 income tax cut seemed to work—the economy boomed for several years—and it has entered into the lore of tax policy as smart fiscal management.

There was, however, another tax tinker—one that failed and, although its failure spoke volumes about Keynesian tax theory, has been ignored. It was an income tax surcharge to "correct" the zooming economy that was thought to be the result of the income tax cut in 1964.

Concern about fast growth caused the Keynesians to start lobbying President Johnson for a major tax increase in 1966. Such an increase, they reasoned, would take money out of the hands of business and consumers (where they had just placed it), spending would decelerate, and the boom would be moderated. Although they persuaded Johnson to include a 6 percent surcharge on individual and corporate income taxes in his January 1967 budget message, he did not actually send legislation to Congress until August. By that time, the economy seemed to be in overdrive, so the proposed surcharge rate was bumped up to 10 percent. The economy continued to smoke in 1968—the growth rate shot up, inflation climbed to 4 percent, and interest rates passed their 1966 peak. Johnson signed the surcharge into law in June 1968; it was retroactive to April on individual incomes and to January on corporate incomes.

The economists expected it to slow down the economy. They were wrong. The boom kept booming. Consumer spending did not moderate, but actually increased. Ditto for business spending. Even the housing industry, which had been slow early in 1968, sped right up. Indeed, although it was extended in 1969, the income tax surcharge had no impact. This was a major failure, representing a large setback for the notion of fine-tuning the economy. As Arthur Okun, who became chairman of the Council in 1968, said to interviewers later: "The boom effect proved remarkably stubborn and the experience was a sobering one for many economic diagnosticians, forecasters and policy planners. If I seem sensitive in reviewing the results it is only because I am."

Some argued that the surcharge didn't work because it came two years too late. But another view advanced was that the surcharge didn't work because it was temporary—consumers and businesspeople knew it would be lifted, so they just went right on spending. As later experience with tax policy confirmed, this was a crucial insight.

The third major tax action during the 1960s was the investment tax credit. It was one of the truly ominous acts of policy meddling, and its failure, although it took longer to play out, was exactly what could have been predicted from the experience with the income tax surcharge.

In early 1961, the Kennedy administration proposed an investment tax credit to allow business to claim a credit of 7 percent of the cost of an investment against its tax liabilities. Again, its purpose was to give business incentive to spend money, in this case, by encouraging investment projects that wouldn't otherwise be considered.

For their part, businesspeople didn't think that an investment tax credit would create new investment. Nobody undertakes a project without some signal from the market that the fruits of the investment are wanted. More important, if there was to be tax action, businesspeople preferred accelerated depreciation. They wanted a break on investments they would be making in any event or that had been made already.

Widespread antagonism to the investment tax credit was evident in the Senate hearings before the Finance Committee in April 1962. Well over 100 people testified. Interests as diverse as the National Federation of Grain Cooperatives to the American Newspaper Publishers Association, as the Electronics Industries Association to Walt Disney Productions, were against one provision or another.

Granted, business complaints can sound whiny and selfish, particularly the very specific complaints made against very specific sections of legislation, and some of the complaints might even sound amusing; but that doesn't change the fact that tax legislation has the power to destroy. For example, Richard H. Dickson, president of Indiana Wire & Specialty Company, whose 96-employee firm made point-of-purchase advertising displays, was afraid that a certain subparagraph could be construed to mean that displays were gifts to retailers and thus nondeductible to manufacturers. This, he said, would put his firm out of business.

The chief discontent, however, was with the direction that tax policy was taking. Critics said the bill would be ineffective and worried about possible loss of revenues at a time when the budget was in deficit.

And there were other worries. The treasurer of Halliburton Company, an oil company in Oklahoma, argued: "Normally, we think of tax legislation as having some specific and identifiable purpose, such as increasing revenue, or reducing taxes. Instead it seems to be designed to serve a medley of objectives; namely, the substitution of Government judgment for business judgment and for the free operation of the marketplace." The vice president of Bristol-Myers Company said the tax credit would lead "to the encouragement or discouragement of any particular segment of private enterprise depending upon the whim or mood of the moment." And the National Association of Manufacturers stated: "It would provide a green light for a continued upsweep in Federal spending and a red light against greater and more sustained growth in the private economy."

Simply put, businesspeople were lukewarm about the whole exercise—partly because they felt it set a dangerous precedent for using tax policy as a way of fine-tuning. They proved to be right. The bill became law in October 1962; then along came the Johnson administration and the manipulation of the investment tax credit began.

In 1966, the Johnson administration suspended it, arguing that the suspension was necessary to slow the economy. The point was to reduce business spending so that interest rates would come down, not to raise tax revenue. The treasury secretary, Henry Fowler, told a congressional committee that he was against treating the investment tax credit as a device to be suspended or restored with the normal ups and downs of the economy. And he admitted that when the tax credit passed, the presumption was that it would be permanent. Nonetheless, he went on to say that the current situation was unique and unforeseeable.

Few were convinced. Joel Barlow, speaking for the Chamber of Commerce, which opposed the credit in 1962 on the grounds that it was intended as a short-term device and therefore vulnerable to being suspended or repealed when economic conditions changed, opposed the suspension. He complained that the economists who testified "are talking about problems of economics but they seem oblivious, first, to the necessity for some reasonable certainty, stability, neutrality and simplicity in the tax structure; second, to the hardships and inequities that abound in this sort of on-again, off-again tax legislation; and third, to the mounting taxpayer frustration and impatience which prevents long-range planning."

A spokesperson for the Machinery & Allied Products Institute predicted that the administration's broken promise on making the investment tax credit permanent will make it impossible for any responsible businessperson to assume that the credit won't continue to be subject to change depending on changes in economic conditions. "A substantial part of its incentive impact will thus be lost for good," he said.

The suspension passed and its impact was negative and dramatic, but in an uneven way. The administration's chief economist, Arthur Okun, later said to interviewers: "On long duration equipment, like railroad cars and commercial airplanes, orders just dried up: an 80 percent decrease in orders. On the shelf goods, there was barely any effect. The result was very lopsided. We started getting letters . . . indicating that we were creating huge pockets of unemployment."

Fifteen months later, in March 1966, the administration asked for a suspension of the suspension before the automatic restoration date of January 1, 1968. At the House hearings, Secretary Fowler was back to represent the administration (and grumpy, he told me years later, about again having to defend the investment tax credit as a tool for economic management).

The administration was once more accused of making the investment tax credit "a most flagrant gimmick"—one that compounded the difficulty of making long-term investment plans, didn't belong in the tax code since it was not for raising revenue, and presented the temptation to fiddle with the economy. The restoration of the credit passed. But the damage had been done. Business realized that the tax credit was an awfully flimsy support on which to base investment plans; its reinstatement had little impact.

In 1970, the Nixon administration again eliminated the credit because growth was thought to be too perky. A droopy economy in 1971 prompted the same administration to reinstate it. The economy continued to sag. The Ford administration increased the credit from 7 to 10 percent in 1975. The economy got worse. Whatever investment incentive effect the credit had initially, its yo-yo history swamped it. And, in the end, the policy had became totally ineffective.

All in all, there were nine major tax changes during the 1960s, and only one seemed to work as advertised—the 1964 income tax cut.

During the 1970s, tax policy was relatively passive; there were no major changes, although every other year brought some fiddling with the rates and the creation of little, highly targeted investment tax credits—for research and energy, for example. This relative quiescence was due to a nifty little Catch-22 in which the Keynesians were caught. On the one hand, according to their theory, the sluggish economy suggested tax cuts to perk up spending; on the other hand, according to their theory, climbing inflation suggested tax increases to slow spending. But since the economy was both sluggish and experiencing accelerating inflation, policy was stalemated.

Another, quite sneaky, reason for tax inactivity was due to something called bracket creep: The combination of a steeply progressive tax structure and accelerating inflation kept pushing taxpayers into higher and higher marginal brackets. This nasty little interaction meant that people were paying higher taxes although, in real terms, their incomes had not risen. In fact, by the end of the decade, the middle class faced marginal tax rates of anywhere from 33 to 50 percent. Too bad for taxpayers, but a godsend for official Washington because federal revenues increased without the pain of formally bumping up taxes through legislation.

One notable and amusing tax proposal came out of the 1970s: the Carter administration's $50 income tax rebate. "The $50 rebate was my idea," says chief economist Charles Schultze. "I fought to keep it because the Council didn't want a permanent tax cut." The $50 rebate quickly became a ploy almost as hilarious and just as evanescent as Ford's WIN program—when inflation took a jump early in 1977, the rebate idea was dropped.

In sum, high marginal brackets did nothing to slow inflation, and a maze of investment tax credits did nothing to stimulate economic growth. Both probably did great harm by fleecing citizens and distorting investment decisions—pushing funds into tax-advantaged activities and starving other, more highly taxed investment projects.

Major active tax policy came back into vogue in the 1980s. The chief impetus, and it was a strong one, came from taxpayers who were just plain fed up with high rates. The intellectual force came from a group of tax cutters in the Reagan administration who, like the Keynesians under Kennedy, believed that changes in tax policy constituted the government's most powerful tool for influencing economic growth.

Unlike the Keynesians, however, these policy makers—dubbed supply-siders—dismissed the idea that changes in average rates to promote or discourage spending were important. Rather, they emphasized lower marginal rates, which were at the heart of the incentive effect. It's a simple idea: If people get to keep a larger portion of each extra dollar they earn, they will want to earn more, and thus will work more. Ditto for savers and investors—since the after-tax return on a dollar will go up as the tax rate goes down, so does the incentive to save and invest. In other words, lowering marginal rates would increase incentives to work, save, and invest.

It's difficult to talk about tax policy in the 1980s without a separate word about these supply-siders, especially since many people use the terms "Reaganomics" and "supply-side economics" synonymously—to ridicule, dismiss, or explain policy during President Reagan's tenure.

"Supply-side" was the name used to distinguish the thinking of a disparate bunch of people—a respectable economics professor at Columbia University, a political polemicist in New Jersey, an influential editor at the *Wall Street Journal,* assorted gadflies, and a few bureaucrats at Treasury. It was not a well-integrated argument in the sense that while there was a core belief, there was also lots of disagreement beyond that core.

The core was based on the work of Robert Mundell (the Columbia professor) and popularized by Robert Bartley (the editor of the *Wall Street Journal).* The argument was that monetary and fiscal policy could pull successfully in different directions; for example, the Fed could use tight monetary policy to control inflation and, at the same time, Congress could use stimulative fiscal policy to promote growth. The stimulative side of fiscal policy came from low marginal taxation—which affected incentives to produce, work, and invest—not from the budget deficit.

Beyond that, supply-siders divided over the niceties of monetary policy (how important is it? how tight or loose should it be?), whether exchange rates should be fixed or floating, whether inflation was dangerous, how much government spending should be cut, and what, if any, impact the budget deficit had on interest rates.

Nor was supply-side economics a coherent theory in the way Keynesianism and monetarism were. There wasn't, for instance, a cottage industry of economics professors and graduate students churning out academic papers; indeed, there were only a few rather vague models. Nor was it a new way of looking at the world. The importance of incentives in economic behavior was well-trod territory.

One quick-and-dirty way to characterize supply-side is by the so-called Laffer curve. This, according to a popular story, was the curve drawn on a napkin by economist Arthur Laffer to illustrate the effect of confiscatory tax rates on tax revenue. Laffer didn't invent this curve; rather, it just demonstrated the commonsense trade-off between tax rates and revenues. If the tax rate is zero, then revenues are zero. As rates start to rise, so does revenue, until the point where tax rates are so high that they either discourage the activity that is being taxed or encourage evasion. At that point, tax revenue starts to decline until the point where 100 percent tax rates produce zero revenues.

The point of the curve, of course, is that if marginal tax rates are very high, then lowering them will result in more, not less, revenue. It is not clear whether Laffer and others argued that rates in the United States had reached such a level that a cut would result in more revenue. Although Bartley argues that this interpretation of the Laffer curve was used to discredit the Reagan tax cuts, he also admits that "it was convenient for us to let that point go by." The silence may have been politically expedient, but the result was that when the tax cuts did not result in a deficit-defying surge of revenue, the Laffer curve and supply-side economics were pronounced a failure.

Laffer curve aside, supply-siders were a lot like Keynesians in that they believed in the power of correct policy to deliver a happy economy. Asked to attribute the economic growth achieved in the 1980s, Bartley answers: "The 1980s growth was policy driven. It's pretty clear that the world economy was on the ropes in the beginning of the decade. I suspect we were on the verge of another depression. But the recovery started because of the tax cuts and the Fed's easing."

Of course, Reaganomics wasn't a coherent economic theory, either. Its animus was more vague and more political and proceeded directly from Reagan's dislike of government. The basic belief of the Reaganauts was less government—fewer taxes, less spending (and thus a smaller federal budget, deficit or surplus), and less regulation. The only more was more national defense. Further, it's not clear whether Reagan himself was a supply-sider. Sure, he wanted fewer taxes and lower marginal rates, but he probably never believed in the "convenient" notion that the tax cuts would call forth sufficient revenues to reduce the deficit. As his chief economist, Martin Feldstein, says: "I never heard the president say—and he was always very careful—that the tax cuts would pay for themselves." And Reagan wasn't shy about approving tax hikes when the budget deficit ballooned—which drove the supply-siders nuts.

A broader view would put supply-side economics as part of the overall tax revolt that had begun in the states in the late 1970s and had spread to Washington by the end of the decade. This anti-tax sentiment was broad-based enough to include lots of groups, each calling themselves by different names—even Democrats.

At any rate, both the antitax feeling and the reverence for the power of tax policy resulted in three major tax changes during the 1980s. The first was in 1981, with the Economic Recovery Tax Act (ERTA), which mandated across-the-board cuts in individual marginal income tax rates, to be spread over three years, with a 5 percent reduction followed by two 10 percent cuts. The maximum rate was reduced to 50 percent, and the capital gains rate to 20 percent. The act also provided for the indexing for inflation of tax brackets in 1985 to end bracket creep and for tax-free savings accounts. It also included many, many tax breaks for business—faster write-offs, for instance.

In 1982, however, the endearingly named Tax Equity and Fiscal Responsibility Act (TEFRA) took back a lot of the tax breaks for business granted in ERTA, like liberalized depreciation, and increased many excise taxes.

The second change came in 1983, when, astonishingly, the administration signed off on a big tax increase with the Amendments to the Social Security Act. Coverage was extended to new federal workers and employees of nonprofits, state and local employees were no longer allowed to withdraw from the system, and general revenues were committed to the Social Security Fund. The tax increase scheduled for 1985 was accelerated to 1984 and the rate was scheduled to increase again in 1988. The tax on self-employment earnings went up, and some benefits became taxable. Doubtless, these changes erased a looming deficit in the fund, but they did so by raising taxes—almost 80 percent of the Social Security deficit was reduced by tax increases.

The third change, the Tax Reform Act of 1986, again cut taxes and altered the structure of the federal income tax. The administration argued for it on the grounds that tax revenue generally had remained around 19 to 20 percent of the economy. (True, earlier tax cuts were in part offset by bracket creep before indexation took hold and increases in the Social Security payroll tax.) This tax plan was also a step away from the idea of using tax incentives to manage behavior and toward an idea that had been gaining ground— the tax code ought to promote fairness and a level playing field for investment decisions.

Despite a threatening bulge in the federal budget deficit, almost everybody liked the idea. Witness the *Time* magazine cover in August 1986. In prose unusually breathless, even for *Time*, the copy reads: "They said it couldn't be done. . . . Scrap the gargantuan federal tax code and write a simpler, fairer one? How naive! Drastically reduce top tax rates to their lowest levels in 58 years by throwing out the special breaks and deductions that have accrued over the past four decades? No way! Let the free market determine how people spend and invest their money rather than allow shills for favored industries to use the tax code to tinker with the economy? Get real! Such a drastic overhaul would amount to putting the public interest ahead of special interests. . . ." And, just like the 1981 tax reform, this one had strong bipartisan support in Congress.

The Tax Reform Act of 1986 broadened the personal and corporate income tax base and substantially lowered tax rates. On personal income, 14 brackets, ranging from 11 to 50 percent, were replaced by two brackets of 15 and 28 percent. (The 15 percent bracket and personal exemption were phased out for high-income returns, resulting in an implicit 33 percent bracket.) The tax base was enlarged to include all long-term capital gains, state and local sales tax, IRA contributions for higher incomes, and nonmortgage consumer interest payments.

In an effort to end the maze of taxes that was distorting business and investment decisions, strong limits were placed on tax-sheltered activities, the poor old investment tax credit was repealed yet again, and the capital gains rate was raised from 25 to 28 percent, thus eliminating special treatment for capital gains. Business got its top marginal tax rate lowered from 46 to 34 percent.

The administration argued that these changes would have two major effects. They would improve incentives—specifically, that lower marginal tax rates on personal income would increase the amount that people were willing to work and reduce the attractiveness of tax loopholes; and, second, more uniform rates on income from various capital investments would create a more efficient allocation of investment funds. (When the bill passed Congress, only one amendment was approved: a nonbinding resolution that Congress should not change the tax code for another five years!)

What effect, exactly, did these three major tax changes have on the economy?

Despite all the fussing and fuming on both sides of the debate, tax revenue as a share of the economy hardly moved; indeed, by 1989, revenue as a share of the economy was the same as it was in 1979. Nonetheless, the changes did improve the tax code enormously. Rich people had their marginal rate reduced from 70 percent to less than 34 percent, median-income taxpayers had their marginal rates reduced by a third, and millions of low-income people were freed from any income tax.

As for the touted incentive impact, the record is dim. There was surely more work effort. Most of that came from a stampede of women into the labor force (count that as a positive), but, at the same time, a smaller but significant rush of men left the labor force, many taking the early retirement afforded by changes in Social Security (count that as a negative). So, on balance, one incentive effect was dampened by another.

As for investment, a decadal view shows it mostly unchanged. Gross investment stayed constant as a share of the economy from 1960 to 1990, and net investment continued its previous two-decade trend by falling. The composition of investment, however, did change. Because of 1981 tax changes favorable to real estate, investment in commercial structures zoomed from 22 to 23 percent of net investment in the 1960s and 1970s to over 30 percent in the 1980s. Most of that surge came early in the decade, when ERTA bestowed generous tax breaks for the builders of malls and office buildings. This incentive effect proved so mighty that many of these breaks were later yanked away in the Tax Reform Act of 1986. The rate at which corporations invested in research and development also decelerated after 1985.

The third category in which there were to have been large incentive effects, savings, was an absolute loser. The personal savings rate took a spill: as a percentage of disposable income, it went from a little under 8 percent in the 1970s to around 4.5 percent by the close of the 1980s. And, of course, national savings were created by the federal budget deficit.

In the 1990s, a burst of tax increases decisively reversed the direction of the 1980s. The first was courtesy of the Bush administration, which, despite the very public lips pledge not to do so, did so. Taxes were raised on personal income, bumping up the top rate from 28 percent to 31 percent, and some deductions were taken back. Many excise taxes went up, as did payroll taxes. And, don't forget, this was the occasion for the 10 percent tax on luxury goods.

Next came the Clinton administration, which had promised middle-class tax relief during the presidential campaign. But when its first economic plan, in the form of the budget for 1993, came, there was no tax cut for the middle class; instead, there was a tax hike for "the rich," who saw their marginal income tax rate go from 31 to 36 percent, while the richer-still confronted a 39.6 percent marginal bracket. The Omnibus Budget Reconciliation Act of 1993 also bumped up taxes on Social Security and Medicare benefits.

The disappearing tax cut was especially disappointing because the federal tax burden, including Social Security, corporate, and excise taxes, was back up to 23 percent of average family income, just where it was at the end of the 1970s. And just like the end of the 1970s, taxpayers cried "Tilt!," thereby starting a scramble in Washington to come up with some sort of relief.

But what kind of relief?

On Fantasy Island, it would mean some sort of head tax—paperwork would be minimal, nobody would escape, and individual taxes would be low. In Washington, however, it could mean one of two options: a flat (or flattish) tax on income or a tax on consumption. Both would tax more things but at a lower rate. That's good. But ultimate goodness depends on how far back we are willing to step from the manipulation of the tax system to favor one thing over another. Will homeowners, for example, be willing to give up their mortgage deduction for a lower tax rate?

It would be nice to declare that we have reached an historic moment for our tax code. After all, it is now clear that the problem with trying to devise a system to take advantage of economic incentives created by taxes is that we can't. Experience has demonstrated that the idea only works on paper: The code is packed with carefully crafted taxes that should have had such-and-such an impact but didn't, preferring, once in the real world, to produce various unexpected and suboptimal results. The net effect of these tax laws has been to create a system that fosters confusion, complexity, inefficiency, costliness, inequity.

So perhaps it's time to give up the conceit that the tax system can be used to manage economic behavior in a predictable way. Perhaps it's time to return the tax system to its main goal of raising revenue, and doing so in the simplest, most efficient, fairest way possible.

8

The Federal Budget Deficit

Tolerance of—if not enthusiasm for—deficits in the federal budget was one of the more wacky components of Keynesian theory. Not that federal budget deficits were unheard-of before the Keynesians came to Washington; the budget was often (although modestly) in the red during the 1950s. But, back then, the occurrence of a deficit was always viewed as lamentable and temporary. The Keynesians set out to change this attitude.

Their argument was that deficits were an excellent way to stimulate economic growth: when consumer and/or business spending sagged, causing the business cycle to hit a drag period, government could ride to the rescue by injecting a little spending of its own, especially if that spending created or enlarged a budget deficit.

This was thought to be a very high-powered solution to the problem of slow growth because government spending sets off a chain of respending. First government injects money into the economy, say by giving funds to builders for highway construction; the highway builders use the funds to buy labor and materials; the workers and material suppliers in turn spend their money on food or cars or whatever; the sellers of the whatevers, in turn, spend their money on other whatevers. Of course, the whole portion is not respent each time—at each link in the chain, some money is retained for savings or goes back to government in form of taxes. But the ultimate impact of the respending is much greater than the initial amount (hence the term "multiplier").

This chain was said by Keynesians to be much more high-powered if government has to borrow the money it injects into the economy; that is, if the spending were undertaken even though government didn't have sufficient funds for it. After all, what's debt to the federal government? There is no need for government to pay down its debt; it can keep rolling it over. In this view, government deficit spending is a little like funny money except it goes into the economy to buy real goodies. Ditto for tax cuts. When the government "returns" money to taxpayers—or allows money to be "retained"—that money is also spent and respent. Thus, an economic downturn can be countered by a tax cut that engenders a chain of respending, especially when the tax cut creates a shortfall in the federal budget.

From the Keynesian perspective, both government spending and tax cuts were okay in generating a deficit, but since government spending was easier to achieve politically, it became the main slugger for policy.

Keynesians even went so far as to distinguish between two types of budget deficits: those that were the natural result of slow growth and those that were undertaken deliberately to speed growth. Consider the language in the 1963 *Economic Report* that put the Keynesian argument bluntly. Kennedy's letter stated that actual U.S. output of goods and services were running well below the economy's potential capacity to produce, and that the pace of expansion would not accelerate until the tax cuts took hold. "So until we restore full prosperity and the budget balancing revenues it generates, our practical choice is not between deficit and surplus but between two kinds of deficits: deficits born of waste and weakness and deficits incurred as we build our future strength."

Since the sticking point about budget deficits for the public and business was that they might cause inflation, the Kennedy administration sought to reassure by instructing readers that prices rise when demand exceeds supply, not as the result of deficits. Public, you have a choice, they said. Continue with these flabby, unproductive deficits—deficits born of ignorance and weakness— or seize the day and let us run strong, powerful deficits. Either keep to your benighted anxieties and suffer an inferior economy or let us run a deliberate deficit and show you what a manly government can do. Inflation? Don't be silly. Not from our kind of deficits.

In fact, as it turned out, there was only one kind of deficit— flabby and unproductive. Three decades of experience with year after year of deficits, and the consequent swelling of the national debt, has demonstrated that deficits do not prevent, or even shorten, down periods in the business cycle. The country has endured some stinging recessions despite big deficits; during the 1970s, the economy sagged even though the budget showed a deficit; it slumped again in the early 1990s with large deficits and grew in the mid-1990s with smaller deficits. It is clear that federal budget deficits do not spur economic growth.

It is also clear that running constant deficits is not good policy. For starters, eventually they will cause inflation and/or interest rates to be higher than they otherwise might be.

Since a budget deficit is the result of the government spending more money than it takes in through taxes, it has to borrow money. The Treasury borrows this money by issuing debt securities (U.S. bonds, bills, or notes). At any time, there are all sorts of debt securities in the market, mostly varieties of government and corporate paper, but government securities are thought to be the "best buy" because they carry very, very little risk of default.

Now comes the tricky part. Buyers of those Treasury debt securities can consist of the public (private investors) or another part of government (the Federal Reserve). If the buyers of the government debt are private investors, then interest rates will tend to rise and these higher interest rates will crowd out private investment. This is called crowding out because government debt has attracted private savings and forced private debtors either to raise interest rates on their debt to compete with government debt or drop out of the market. (In other words, federal debt crowds some investment out of the market.) If, on the other hand, the buyer is the Federal Reserve, which pays for its purchase by injecting more money into the banking system, then inflation might result. This is called monetizing the debt because the government has, in a sense, printed money to buy its own debt.

Thus, the result of government debt issuance can be either higher interest rates or higher rates of inflation—or both.

Another problem with deficit spending, one that wasn't even recognized by Keynesians, is that deficits and the national debt are a burden borne by future generations. The old Keynesian excuse, that the debt wasn't important because "we owe it to ourselves," doesn't hold because the "ourselves" who benefit are not the same selves who have to contend with the consequences. If deficits cause higher interest rates, then the interest costs of the debt will rise in the future. If deficits crowd out private investment, then there will be a smaller capital stock and the economy will be less productive in the future. And succeeding generations will face higher interest costs and have less income to pay them. At some point, future generations will see their taxes go up or the services they receive from government spending cut. The deficits are actually a sign that "ourselves" are spending our children's money.

A third difficulty with deficits is that government spending in the service of generating deficits proved to have an awesome ratchet effect. Once a government spending program was created and funding begun, it was almost impossible to stop. Not only were benefits expanded, but the number of recipients rose, either from the natural population growth or the expansion of eligibility. That was surely true of entitlement spending such as Social Security, Medicare, and Medicaid (both of which started at modest levels in 1965).

Hence, in the 1960s, government spending represented about 19 percent of economic activity. In the 1970s, the government was spending 23 percent of the economy. And in the 1980s, despite growing unhappiness with government spending, it averaged almost 24 percent of economic activity. Entitlements grew from under 30 percent of federal spending to a peak of 50 percent in 1975; they fell slightly during the 1980s, but were back to over 50 percent by 1993.

And, finally, the ability to run constant deficits results in a sort of carefree attitude on the part of government on how the funds are spent. Hence the proliferation of spending on programs and projects that are wasteful.

At any rate, back in the 1960s, most of these problems were only dimly sighted, if in view at all. So the experiment with deliberate deficits was tried: the federal budget came up short in 1961, 1962, 1963, and 1964. The economy logged good growth. The theory looked like a winner. *Time* magazine, in December 1965, remarked that businesspeople had been persuaded that deficit spending is not immoral. "Nor, perhaps in the greatest change of all, do they believe that the Government will ever fully pay off its debt any more than General Motors or IBM find it advisable to pay off their long-term obligations." The budget was in deficit 1965, 1966, 1967, and 1968. In 1969, a budget surplus was the last one achieved in recent memory.

As a share of the economy, the budget deficit was never more than around 3 percent until 1975. Then the real trouble began. It was during the Ford administration when a slow economy prompted Ford to abandon his fiscal conservatism in favor of deficit spending—producing what turned out to be the largest peacetime deficit to that moment, measuring 3.5 percent of the economy. During that year, Congress increased both the size of Ford's tax cut and amount of federal spending. Both Ford and his chief economist, Alan Greenspan, were upset about the prospect of a ballooning deficit. Greenspan was pessimistic about the stimulus part of the program because of the "increase in negative expectation" generated by the deficit; he said later, "I was unhappy with the deficit, it was the beginning of the real erosion." The deficit grew to a 4.4 percent share of the economy.

The Carter administration came into office promising to reduce the deficit to zero. It did manage to reduce the relative share of the federal budget deficit, but that was achieved with record taxes of 22.4 percent of the economy, the highest share in history. Taxes notwithstanding, and although estimates from future tax revenues showed that the budget would be in balance for 1981, deficits logged in at nearly 3 percent of the economy for both 1980 and 1981.

In the 1980s, the words "budget surplus" became an oxymoron, and "budget deficit" became one word and a way of life. It was also the moment when opinion turned against the desirability of running deficits in the federal budget. When the deficit surged to over 6 percent of the economy in 1983, people (and policy makers) began to realize that deficits weren't something that could be waved away overnight. There was widespread anxiety that deficits were out of control; that they represented profligate government spending (especially for programs that didn't seem to add value to national economic life); and that they were not a tool for achieving sound economic growth.

The Reagan administration, which presided over these large budget deficits, came in for a lot of grief. Critics blamed the administration for fudging the facts; that is, for using "rosy scenarios" of economic growth and promises that aggressive tax cutting would increase tax revenue. Reaganites, for their part, blamed the deficits on Congress's inability to rein in government spending. Who was right?

A look at the numbers supports the administration's point that the swollen deficit was a consequence of escalating government spending. During the 1980s, government spending increased in real terms (in 1985, government spending represented a huge 24.4 percent share of economic activity), while, during the same period, tax revenue remained at about the same share of the economy as it was in 1979. That suggests that federal budget deficits were due not to declining tax revenue, but to an inability to control the growth of government spending.

On the other hand, there is no question that the administration's growth estimates were excessive and no question that the budget deficit ballooned bigger than forecast. To be fair, however, almost all administrations are optimistic about growth. And the Reagan economists did end up downgrading their estimates a little bit each year.

As for the other charge—that the administration claimed that the tax cuts would so increase economic activity and thus tax revenue that the budget deficit would disappear—there is no evidence. As William Niskanen, a member of the Council at the time, says firmly, "The administration never suggested that tax cuts would increase revenues; that was an invention of the press."

The administration can be faulted, however, for not taking the deficits seriously. From the start, its rhetoric about budget deficits was unconvincing. Although the economists got the drill right, arguing that since deficits impose costs on the economy by either crowding out private investment or prompting inflationary money creation, and since deficits also impose a cost on future generations through higher taxes or a lower level of government services, the budget should be balanced. Further, the economists promoted a balanced budget as a way of containing the growth of government and assuring people of future government restraint. Nonetheless, like other administrations before it, the Reaganites did not think that a balanced budget was something to be rushed into. Rather, since taxes were being reduced before spending cuts were made, the administration acknowledged that it would "take some time" to achieve a balanced budget.

In any case, in 1983, when the deficit reached an all-time high as a share of the economy, at over 6 percent, the administration refused to raise taxes or cut defense spending, but demanded that Congress cut other government spending. Congress refused. The administration pointed out that over the past 20 years, outlays for nondefense programs had nearly doubled as a share of the economy. It scolded the government for taking more and more of people's income and tossing it away on programs that, however well intentioned, actually aggravated the problems they set out to solve.

As for its own stepped-up spending on defense, however, the administration said that since it had cut nondefense spending, excluding Social Security and Medicare, as a percent of the economy, it had leeway to increase defense spending without increasing taxes. At least that's the argument. And a silly one it is, considering that spending on Social Security and Medicare was mushrooming.

By 1984, however, the administration admitted that despite

their best efforts at snipping spending, the country still faced years of deficits that could not be "grown" out of. And so, in 1985, with the deficit at 5.4 percent of the economy, the administration was ready to endorse what Reagan economist Bill Niskanen calls "an act of political desperation"—the Gramm-Rudman-Hollings Balanced Budget and Emergency Deficit Control Act.

The Gramm-Rudman Act phased in deficit reductions over five years so that the budget would be balanced by 1991. It required automatic spending cuts if Congress did not produce sufficient deficit reductions; the cuts were to be taken in a 50-50 share between defense and nondefense spending, but certain items were exempt: Social Security, Medicare, and congressional salaries. (As it turned out, automatic cuts were imposed in 1986, 1988, and 1990, but they were tiny and didn't last very long.)

In 1987, the deficit as a share of the economy showed real improvement, dropping to under 4 percent. (Nonetheless, this was also the year that the Gramm-Rudman targets were revised to hit a zero budget deficit in 1993, instead of 1991.) And, by 1989, the deficit had sunk to 2.9 percent of the economy, the lowest mark since 1981.

But then came the Bush administration. It delivered what was billed as a budget-balancing budget in 1990, which consisted mostly of raising taxes (and, oddly, dropping the Gramm-Rudman targets entirely). But the budget deficit as a share of the economy began rising again, back to over 4 percent. Why? Because the administration let government spending boom. Between 1989 and 1993, spending went from the 22 percent share of economic activity logged during the last two years of the Reagan administration to over 23 percent.

The Clinton administration enjoyed a brief respite from deficit problems. The economic recovery and a big tax increase bumped up revenues, spending subsided to a tad over 22 percent of the economy, and the deficit dropped to 3.1 percent of the economy by 1994. (This good news is temporary, however. Projections show that after 1996, the deficit will streak into the stratosphere, fueled by rapidly rising entitlement spending on Social Security, Medicare and Medicaid.)

All these ups and downs, figures, targets, and projections aside, the fact remains that there have been over 30 years of budget deficits. And those years have now generated an angry consensus that government deficit financing has to end.

It has failed utterly as a device to manage the economy. Through these 30 years of deficits, the business cycle has continued its undulations: the existence of budget deficits has not stimulated economic activity sufficiently to avoid troughs. Too, budget deficits have drained funds from the national savings pool. And government's huge share of those funds has been often directed to uses that do not represent the best, or highest, return. Deficit financing has not only actually put upward pressure on prices, but, in addition, the possibility that deficits will be financed through excess money creation keeps the financial markets jumpy over inflation. Moreover, deficit financing has come to represent an ever-increasing debt to future generations—the national debt was almost $5 trillion in 1994 and interest payments consumed 16 percent of the federal budget.

Hence, the idea of a constitutional amendment requiring a balanced federal budget has become attractive. It seems to enjoy not only public support but a bit of political determination as well.

Yet, even if such an amendment were achieved, there will be problems. From a purely economic standpoint, many worry that maintaining a zero budget deficit during recessions is too rigid— that the economy needs a little leeway for government spending to cheer up a drooping economy. After all, during a downturn, demand for government funds, such as unemployment benefits, goes up while financial wherewithal, such as tax revenue, goes down. The fear is that the financial rigor needed to balance the budget under these trying circumstances will make those circumstances worse.

A second, less noble, class of anxieties has to do with the ever-present possibility of political hanky-panky. Creative accounting may produce budgets that balance only on paper, and escape clauses may render even that paper achievement useless.

And a third fear is that there is no real way to enforce such an amendment. If Congress does not match revenue with spending, what's the punishment? A lecture from the Supreme Court? A midnight visit by U.S. marshals? And just who, exactly, would be held accountable?

These anxieties aside, the biggest problem is how to get there from here. Raising taxes is not the answer; it has been tried and tried and each time the government spends the extra bucks. The only answer is to cut government spending and to cut it decisively. The next biggest problem is where to cut.

Here's how the government spending pie sliced in 1994: 22 percent went for Social Security, 18 percent for defense, 15 percent for interest on the debt, 10 percent for Medicare, and 6 percent for Medicaid; this represented about 70 percent of the total. Interest on the debt cannot be cut, and many feel that the share going to defense is already about as low as is prudent. And here is where the heart of the problem beats. Obviously, the most desirable place to cut is also the most politically dangerous—entitlements.

At current growth rates, in eight years, Social Security, Medicare, and Medicaid will constitute almost half of the federal budget. But it is not only sheer size that makes these entitlement programs enticing to serious budget cutters. Two of them (Social Security and Medicare) are subsidies to the middle class and thus could be reduced without causing terrible hardship. And therein lies the political rub. The middle class may not want to forsake their entitlements and they will punish at the polls those who make them do so.

Simply put, if an amendment mandating balanced budgets is violated, there will be many candidates to punish and a lot of otherwise nice and law-abiding people could expect a midnight visit from federal marshals. Nonetheless, it's worth a try.

9

Regulation

Government regulation is invidious: It dampens productivity, saps innovation, damages business investment, creates uncertainty, costs a lot of money, promotes frustration, supports two insufferable groups—lawyers and bureaucrats—and drives otherwise sensible people mad.

So why do we have so much of it?

Well, a lot of the problem is that opportunities to regulate are everywhere. Almost any activity qualifies when you consider that the manufacture of goods or the provision of services can be overseen—everything from big ticket items like putting import quotas on cars to small-beer events like requiring a permit to hunt deer. Temptations multiply.

A second reason is that the stated goals of regulation are attractive. Who doesn't want to breathe clean air and climb safe ladders? Moreover, while the benefits might be clear, the costs are often hidden. It's easy for the government to impose regulations because costs are mostly paid by business (which pass them on to consumers as higher prices, or employees as lower salaries, or shareholders as lower returns). Simply put, while the ultimate costs are often indirect, the federal government can reap the direct benefit of looking good.

Finally, there are mighty establishments attached to regulatory activities. Worker bees in the government put food on the table by enforcing regulations, lawyers and accountants get theirs by figuring them out and helping people either to comply with or evade them. You won't hear many complaints from these beneficiaries about the burdens of their life's work.

Hence, government has always been an eager regulator in social and economic affairs. Unfortunately, however, regulation is another facet of the delusion that government is the most powerful and enlightened player in economic life, a Superman of Good Outcomes. So beyond the obvious problems associated with regulation are the less obvious but no less troublesome ones of unintended consequences, uncertainty, and gridlock. Pollution controls for automobiles, for example, push up the cost of new cars so that drivers stick with their old cars longer, thereby actually increasing pollution.

In the 1960s, regulatory efforts were mostly aimed at cleanliness: the Clean Air Act in 1963, Motor Vehicle Air Pollution Control Act in 1965, Air Quality Act in 1967, Water Quality Act of 1965, and the Solid Waste Disposal Act of 1965. By and large, these were modest in scope and cheap compared with what came later.

In the 1970s, regulation was awarded academic respectability when the government added to its task of managing the economy (macroeconomics) the responsibility of fixing something called market failures (the realm of microeconomics), and regulatory focus shifted to social regulation—an attempt to correct market failures in areas like the environment, safety, and health.

A market failure occurs when there is a gap between the private and social costs of an activity. That is, the social costs are higher than the private costs. The activity itself is something economists call an externality. For example, consider a factory where the production process throws off disgusting waste. If the factory dumps this junk into a handy river instead of disposing it in a less convenient, less harmful place, the resulting pollution is an externality.

Of course, the problem is that by using the river as a dump, production costs are lower than if the factory disposed of its waste in a socially responsible way, so the factory owner has little incentive not to pollute. This leaves the people and businesses living along the river, who suffer the bad effects, to bear the cost—hence the term "social cost."

The failure of the market to cover the costs of an externality is taken as an invitation for the government to step in and make private parties deal with the social costs. In this example, the government could promulgate regulations to stop river pollution by making it unlawful for the factory to dump waste in the river, which, in turn, would raise the private cost of production but lower the social costs borne by society.

At any rate, during the 1970s, the "correction" of market failures accelerated the pace of social regulation. In 1970, both the Occupational Safety and Health Act and the Clean Air Act were passed. Two years later came the Marine Protection Act, the Water Pollution Act, and the Federal Insecticide and Rodenticide Act. These were followed by the Safe Drinking Water Act in 1974 and the Toxic Substances Control Act of 1975. There were also amendments to the Clean Air Act in 1977. A welter of new bureaucracies were created, among others: the Environmental Protection Agency, the Occupational Safety and Health Administration, the Consumer Product Safety Commission, and the National Highway Traffic Safety Administration.

The extravaganza continued in the 1980s. In environmental regulation, more than half a dozen laws were passed, including the Radon Gas and Indoor Air Quality Research Act in 1986; the Radon Pollution Control Act in 1988; the Clean Air Amendments in 1990; CERCLA (the Comprehensive Environmental Response, Compensation and Liabilities Act—the notorious Superfund) in 1980; the Hazardous and Solid Waste Amendments in 1984; FIFRA (the Federal Insecticide, Fungicide, and Rodenticide Act Amendments) in 1988.

Nineteen ninety was a stellar year for regulatory excess. First came the mother of expensive regulation—additional amendments to the Clean Air Act. The law, which covers many businesses from giant utilities and auto companies to tiny bakeries and dry cleaners, could cost as much as $60 billion annually when fully implemented in the late 1990s. Then came the Disabled Americans Act, which requires owners of private businesses, stores, hotels, restaurants, and apartments to make specified physical modifications to accommodate the disabled. The initial conversion costs to bring these establishments into compliance range between $60 billion and $70 billion. There was also legislation requiring food manufacturers to affix labels to products carrying various nutritional information.

A good guide to assessing the growth of regulation is to look at the number of pages in the *Federal Register,* where all new regulations are published annually. Pages went steadily up during the 1970s, until they reached an all-time high of 87,000 in 1979. Indeed, not until the 1980s was there a respite, when the Reagan administration seriously slowed the trajectory of ever more regulation—the number of pages in the *Federal Register* actually declined by 34,000, the amount of federal workers involved in regulation fell, and the cost of administering federal regulatory programs was about flat.

Then the great reversal. During the first two years of the Bush administration, regulation got out of hand. The number of pages in the *Federal Register* increased to 70,000. The number of federal employees busy issuing and enforcing the stuff reached an all-time high of almost 125,000, and the amount of money devoted to administering these programs grew at double-digit rates. It got so bad, in fact, that, in 1992, Bush had to announce a regulatory reform against his own administration—no new rules for 90 days, later extended another 90 days. No matter. In came the Clinton administration and the growth of new pages resumed apace.

There is no one correct and clear way to measure the cost of regulation on the economy. But there are plenty of estimates. One of the most reasonable figures is that in 1992, regulation cost one-half trillion dollars, or 1 percent of the economy. This figure includes social regulation such as environment, health, and safety; economic regulation like trade restrictions, federal labor laws, and farm programs; and the paperwork involved in filling out forms, keeping records, paying accountants and lawyers.

This last category deserves special mention. The $7 billion budget of the IRS is a scintilla compared with the private (business and individual) cost of the figuring and filling out tax forms of almost $200 billion a year. The labor of those who must wade through the paperwork involved in health care reimbursement accounts for over $30 billion a year. (As might be expected with three decades of growing regulation, the number of lawyers ballooned—indeed, lawyers per capita more than doubled over this period.)

In general, the cost of regulating is initially expressed as a cost of doing business. Okay, but who pays this tariff? We all do, in one way or another.

Consider a standard situation in which a law requires certain practices to be followed in hiring or procedures to be used to assure product quality. The former will raise costs by forcing employers to expand their job search and fill out forms to prove compliance, the latter will raise costs by requiring changes in the production process. Sometimes, firms can pass these costs to consumers, making them pay more; sometimes, firms can't pass them along at all, so they will have lower profits, which means that owners or shareholders foot the bill. But, often, employers can pass these costs down the line with lower wages and salaries. Other times, when costs cannot be directly passed off to employees, employers will respond by either hiring fewer people or laying off those already employed. Either way, higher business costs from regulation will result in lower wages and/or higher unemployment.

There are also situations well beyond individual employers' control. For example, environmental regulations like those protecting certain birds or fish can result in the shrinkage of entire industries, like logging and fishing.

Excessive regulation also discourages investment in domestic business; why plop a factory down on regulated soil when unregulated opportunities beckon abroad? Moreover, the threat of regulatory changes creates uncertainty, which scares investors, who then demand higher returns, and tends to make planning horizons more short-term.

Further, regulation stymies innovation. This has been especially true in the drug and medical-device industry. Long approval periods shorten the effective patent time for the results of expensive research and development and thus diminish returns on discoveries without lowering risk. A larger gap between risk and return renders many research and development projects too unprofitable to undertake.

And, last, all of the above make it harder for domestic firms to compete in international markets in which many foreign-based firms to do not have to contend with the effects of excessive regulation.

What makes all the direct and indirect costs, to say nothing of the mind-numbing frustration, even more wicked, is that taken all together, these costs slow economic growth. Rather than detailing the many subtle ways in which regulation impedes growth that are so favored by economists, here instead is just one basic example. Innovation requires research, but research might not be undertaken if regulation makes the fruit of that research susceptible to liability action. Innovation requires development, but development might not be undertaken if regulation draws out the period before approval is granted. In other words, firms need a secure environment for innovation before they will commit money, time, and other scarce resources to the process. Lacking that environment, there will be less business innovation, which leads to slower productivity growth, and that creates slower economic growth.

There are, of course, offsetting benefits to regulation, especially those that concern health and safety. People are less susceptible to sickness, injury, and death because of the many workplace and drug and food laws. Ditto for those who fly airplanes and drive cars. And certainly everybody who breathes the air, or swims in rivers or lakes, is better off than they would be if cities still generated dense smogs of pollution or waterways still caught on fire. But no respectable effort has been made to quantify these benefits overall.

It is, however, possible to estimate benefits in specific categories. For example, trade restrictions such as quotas on imported cars or textiles benefit the workers who keep their jobs—so just multiply the number of jobs "kept" by annual salaries to arrive at total benefit. The irony is that often when these benefits are quantified, the costs of the regulations outweigh them. For example, the total figure for the benefits from restricting imports that accrue to domestic car and textile industries, in profits and jobs, is smaller than the costs to consumers in the form of higher prices for cars and clothes.

Then there are categories that don't seem to produce any benefits at all. Consider, for instance, the billions of dollars needed to remove asbestos from buildings, although the very removal may be as health-threatening as if the stuff were just left alone, or the billions it costs to clean up hazardous-waste sites, despite the lack of evidence that those sites constitute a hazard. And, finally, there are categories in which regulation actually results in negative benefits—that is, in harm. The Food and Drug Administration, for instance, has delayed approval of many drugs and medical devices that could have saved lives; critics point to long approval times (measured in years) for Interleukin 2 for kidney cancer, for example.

For any readers isolated from the impact of regulatory zeal and therefore of the mind that I am overstating the case, there exists a real world example of the positive impact of unraveling regulation. Consider the move in the 1970s to deregulate large sectors of the economy. This economic event was aimed at freeing a few very basic industries in the country's infrastructure—some of which had been seriously regulated as far back as the 19th century.

It was no little irony that at the same time the government was busy formulating standards for hundreds of millions of products and activities from breakfast cereal to bicycles, and thereby intruding in everyday life in an unprecedented way, it decided to undertake a major and important effort to reverse some earlier regulatory efforts. But the time was ripe: The notion that excessive regulation was slowing productivity, adding to inflation and generally impeding economic growth, had been kicking around in academic economics for some time. Slow economic growth in the 1970s convinced many nonacademics that the notion might be correct.

A real breakthrough came in 1975 when President Ford, asking Congress for fundamental changes in the laws regulating transportation—railroads, airlines, and trucking firms—used the word "cost" to discuss regulation. Ford complained that "regulation has been used to protect and support the growth of established firms rather than to promote competition." And he pointed to the proliferation of commissions, agencies, bureaus, and offices to oversee new programs and the cumbersome and costly procedures to license, certify, review, and approve of new technologies and products.

This spirit continued in force under Carter—along with deregulation of transportation, there were major steps to deregulate the financial markets and telecommunications, and to decontrol energy prices. Early in his tenure, Carter was apparently impressed by the argument that an increase in regulation showed up as cost increases followed by price increases and ultimately as wage increases. In the 1978 *Economic Report,* Carter wrote: "There is no question that the scope of regulation has become excessive and that too little attention is given to its economic costs . . . wherever possible, the extent of regulation should be reduced." True to his word, in 1978 came the Airline Deregulation Act and a strong push for similar deregulation in trucking and rails. In 1979, Carter presented deregulation bills for telecommunications and financial services.

Deregulation of these infrastructure industries was the most significant policy event of the 1970s—and surely an important one in providing a long-term boost to the economy in the 1980s. Total benefits to the economy are probably around $40 billion a year. Consumers pay lower prices, enjoy more choices and better quality in goods and services from the deregulated industries, and the rate of economic growth has been much stronger than it would have been absent this effort.

But, sadly, just as the benefits of deregulation were being felt, the effort ended. The Reagan administration did not press the agenda forward. Too bad, but even worse, the financial sector was allowed to limp on in a partially deregulated state, creating one of the worst messes in recent history—the savings and loan industry debacle. In fact, what happened to that industry is an almost perfect illustration of how regulation can distort and destroy everything in its path. Kind of a Godzilla consisting of bureaucrats, lobbyists, and crooks.

The idea behind the deregulation of the financial industry was not a bad one. Indeed, it was clear by the 1970s that something had to be done. The industry had been set in stone in the 1930s by laws and regulations that restricted institutions from competing with each other. Commercial banks, savings and loans, brokerage houses, investment banks, and insurance companies were given monopolies on certain forms of business and then cartelized to prevent even intramural competition. The structure had grown so rigid that it was barely able to cope with the modern financial environment of electronic transfer of funds and high and volatile interest rates.

Deregulation of the financial industry began in 1980 when a bunch of rules—like Reg Q, which set interest rate ceilings on savings deposits—began to be phased out. The Reagan administration strongly supported the introduction of competition, arguing that the ability of banks and thrifts to offer insured accounts that were competitive with money market funds in terms of both interest rates and services would heighten the incentive for saving. Perhaps. But the problem was that the administration was supporting more competition in the financial industry while continuing to shelter some of its institutions from the risk that competition brings. In short, as many observers and players warned, the problem with deregulation was not deregulation but the way in which it was being undertaken.

The main case in point was the failure to reform federal deposit insurance. The banking system works only if banks maintain their reputation for safety and convenience. In olden days, for example, when banks were considered risky propositions, one bank failure usually led to panic, other bank failures, and a credit contraction. The Federal Deposit Insurance Act of 1933 changed all that by providing insurance for deposits. The act worked admirably. Lots of banks have failed since 1933, but no one mishap has led to a run on innocent banks.

Sounds fine, but this insurance system, when mixed with competition, led to perverse incentives and the waves of expensive bank failures throughout the 1980s. Consider: The premiums that banks pay for this insurance was not based on the investments in individual portfolios but levied at a fixed rate. Hence, banks with riskier investments pay the same premiums as banks with sound ones. But since banks with riskier portfolios can be more profitable, and since fixed-rate premiums mean there is no penalty for following a high-risk strategy, banks have incentives to behave like high rollers. In short, deposit insurance encourages banks to pursue high-return strategies at the expense of sound ones.

Nor does deposit insurance generate any incentives for depositors to punish banks for undertaking risky investments. If their deposits were not insured, of course, depositors might withdraw their money. But the safety net of insurance shelters depositors from the risk associated with high returns on their accounts.

Anyway. What happened was a textbook case in its predictability. Banks competed for funds by offering depositors high interest rates that they, in turn, provided by investing in high-risk, high-return projects. When the projects turned sour, the government bailed out the banks as a "cheaper" alternative to shutting them down. When bailouts didn't work, depositors turned to the federal government for their money. The eventual cost will be in the hundreds of billions of dollars.

Were the Reagan administration's economists sleeping at the switch? You bet. Here's what they said in the 1983 *Economic Report*. Responding to criticism that competitive pressure might cause thrifts to make high-risk, high-return investments (like junk bonds) in order to offer high interest rates to depositors, the economists wrote: "Even if such claims were true, it does not follow that restricting competition will necessarily improve quality or safety. Moreover there are more direct ways of addressing these potential market defects." Fine. But after this backhanded reference, the subject is dropped. As economics chief Martin Feldstein said a decade later: "We were guilty on Federal deposit insurance. We just did not focus on it."

The administration did begin to worry out loud in 1984, after a bunch of bank failures and the prospect of even more became apparent. It acknowledged the widespread activity of deposit brokers who were slicing large deposits into smaller, insurable amounts and then parceling them out to high-risk, high-return banks all over the country. As banks collapsed, many solutions were noted: tying insurance premiums to risk, upping capital requirements, increasing the risk exposure of large depositors by reducing the amount covered by deposit insurance, and strengthening disclosure requirements and/or privatizing all or part of the insurance system. But no action was even contemplated.

Two years later, in the 1986 *Economic Report*'s obligatory chapter on the virtues of deregulation, there is a discussion of the growing problems stemming from banking deregulation. It is a complete fudge. First, the Council pretended that the fact that hundreds of thrifts were in deep, deep trouble (over 400 banks with assets over $100 billion were insolvent) had little to do with deregulation, saying that this period of difficulty just happens to coincide with deregulation (*quel* coincidence!) and that this "coincidence of deregulation with the problems of some financial institutions has led to the suggestion that deregulation is somehow responsible for these problems."

Rather, the administration argued that the problems of these thrifts were due to too much regulation and volatile rates of inflation. Two possible solutions were suggested—having risk-adjusted deposit insurance and risk-adjusted capital requirements—but then rejected. The only possibility admitted was a path not taken—the prompt closing of insolvent banks, letting the shareholders, big depositors, and managers take a bath. In the end, the economists retreated to the highest possible plane, urging that policy be geared at keeping inflation and interest rates stable because "life is risky enough without macroeconomic policy introducing additional uncertainty." Right as rain, but pretty lame.

And thus did the failure to complete financial deregulation result in a high rate of bank failures and a gigantic bill to close insolvent banks in the 1990s. This seems especially sorry since the successful deregulation of the other industries shows it can be done wisely, safely, and with good economic effect.

In fact, most of the (global) experience with deregulation has been so positive that some people think we should deregulate everything in sight. Should we? There are two equally appealing answers: yes and no. Yes, because of all the bad things that regulation does as argued above. No, because notwithstanding all those bad things, people have already made their adjustments and expect to operate in a regulated environment; a sudden deregulation would create all sorts of new problems.

As attractive as both yes-and-no responses are, however, they don't offer a good guide for future regulation. Since the yen to regulate things—and to hope for good outcomes—is not going to go away, we should figure out some way to regulate while limiting the damage that will surely result.

Take the category that offers the smallest contribution to social welfare and the largest amount of per capita suffering—paperwork. A good approach would be to cut paperwork requirements in half (at least) and then maintain that number—of pages of forms—no matter what. If new paperwork is mandated by some new rule-making outburst, then the same number of pages of old paperwork would have to go. Ipso facto. (We could take a giant step toward a reduction simply by changing the federal income tax system to a flat rate system so that the tax form could fit on a postcard.)

Second, consider economic regulation—the category that is the most unnecessary and is aimed almost exclusively at cheering up special interests. We could just drop it entirely. What's the good of having the discipline of the market if we won't let the market discipline? Minimum wages? Free employers to pay employees based on the value of their work, not on the political calculations of Congress. Trade protection? Let firms and industries fail if they can't cut the mustard internationally. Farm supports and other forms of economic welfare? Dismantle them.

Finally, what about the most expensive category—the one that, no surprise, turns out to have the biggest, most enthusiastic constituency—social regulation. There are plenty of ideas on how to make social regulation more cost-effective. Two are neat variations on the theme of making the feds put its money near its mouth: making the government fund mandates to state and local governments and compensate owners for taking property for other uses (for example, by declaring the property inviolate as wetlands or as having historic interest).

Currently, the most fashionable idea for reform of social regulation is something called risk assessment or risk management. It attacks the presumption behind most social regulation—especially for environmental rules—that risk is controllable. That if breathing bad air or eating apples sprayed with pesticide increases the risk of cancer, then decreasing air pollution or banning pesticides will cut down on that risk.

Fine. Except what if the cost of reducing risk was a million times the benefit derived? Or what if the cost of reducing risk was reasonable, but the risk itself was trivial? Or if the risk itself was grave, but the amount it could be reduced was trivial? Under any of these conditions, would it still make sense to go ahead and regulate?

That's where risk assessment comes in. Using what its proponents like to call sound science or good economics, the risk of a particular activity is measured against the cost of reducing it. And, presumably, if the costs and/or benefits are way out of whack, the regulation will not be undertaken.

There are lots of problems with this approach—beyond the obvious of defining "sound" science or "good" economics—like how to quantify human life, since human life is what is at risk. But requiring a risk assessment investigation before approving new regulations would be a start toward reversing over 35 years of indulging an attitude most easily characterized as "Eek! Look, a risk! Let's regulate it away—right this minute—no matter the cost—hurry!"

Part IV

Why Big, Busy Government Cannot Keep Its Promises

10

A Better Idea

As it must be clear by now, an activist government does not work: on the individual level, it constitutes a source of uncertainty and delivers unintended consequences and regulatory frustration; on the more general level, it has generated grave problems for the economy. But beyond observing the obvious, there is a theory that both interprets the interaction between policy and individuals in everyday life, demonstrating why activism cannot work, and explains broad movements in the economy. It is called Rational Expectations or New Classical Economics.

This theory began to take shape during the 1970s, while economic growth was slumping and the mainstream economics profession was being regularly humiliated. Economists, responding to the failures of Keynesianism, began to use advances in mathematical techniques that permitted more sophisticated model building. The result was the development of a major, compelling theoretical challenge to Keynesianism—one that not only explained the failures of government activism but also demonstrated why such activism would always fail.

That challenge, now known as the New Classical Economics (NCE), made its first peep in an article written in 1961 by John Muth. His insight—that people's expectations about the future were rational rather than irrational—struck government activism at its core. If people are irrational, then they expect the future to be like the present. If people are rational, however, they know that the future will be full of surprise and changes and they will alter their behavior to adapt to these changes.

Muth's logic implied that the effectiveness of government action was based on the notion that people would not respond to policy changes. That notion was nonsense. Such policies could not work in the intended way, Muth argued, because people's responses to policy would, in fact, change as their expectations of the future changed. Simply put, government could not "manage" people's behavior in a predictable, constant fashion.

But Muth's revolutionary idea was ignored. The 1960s were, after all, good times, even happy times, and generated lots of optimism about the economy's future. In fact, Muth's insight languished until it was developed, in the early 1970s, by economists Robert Lucas, Edward Prescott, Thomas Sargent, and Neil Wallace.

Keynesianism was, of course, on the theoretical ropes before the New Classical Economics struck. In 1968, a telling blow was delivered against the notion that the Phillips curve described a trade-off between inflation and unemployment—that with the inflation rate at a certain percent, the economy would produce a certain rate of unemployment. Economists Milton Friedman and Edmund Phelps (working independently) argued that there was a natural rate of unemployment—the result of various demographic, institutional, and economic factors—and that unemployment would, in the long run, settle at this natural rate regardless of the rate of inflation.

A natural rate of unemployment meant that any sort of stable, permanent trade-off between inflation and unemployment was impossible. This idea was, of course, contrary to mainstream thinking during the 1960s, when Keynesians hoped to achieve a 4 percent rate of growth in the real economy, a 4 percent rate of unemployment, and a 1 percent rate of inflation by fine-tuning the economy.

Friedman and Phelps denied that monetary stimulus could bring unemployment down below its natural rate for any length of time. Rather, they argued that if inflation is expected, it has no effect on employment. The argument runs like this: Initially, more money in the economy will increase prices so that firms, responding to higher prices and lower real (inflation-adjusted) wages, will hire more people to increase production. Moreover, workers will continue to work even though their real wages have fallen. But once workers expect prices to rise and understand that higher prices reduce their real wages, they will demand higher nominal wages to compensate. But when labor costs go up, firms will cut back on employment. And any increase in employment and production that had been temporarily produced by higher inflation would then vanish, but inflation would remain.

Simply put, attempts to decrease unemployment by increasing inflation will not work because people will not continue to be fooled by price increases. When people learn to anticipate inflation, the trade-off disappears, and repeated attempts to reduce unemployment by inflation will cause the rate of inflation to rise without lowering the rate of unemployment. Too, if the growth in the money supply is the chief cause of inflation, then reduced monetary growth can cut inflation without creating more unemployment.

For the Keynesian orthodoxy, this was remarkable stuff. It

meant that the government had only a magic moment to manage the economy—the moment before expectations caught up to reality. Remarkably, too, this theory was years ahead of experience. The 1968 prediction that the Phillips curve would cease to have any meaning was not actually confirmed until the experience of the 1970s, when inflation and unemployment rose together. Eventually, most Keynesians conceded that the monetarists were correct in asserting that monetary policy has no effect on economic activity in the long run, and that the primary cause of inflation is too much money chasing too few goods.

During the 1970s, as the monetarists emerged victorious in the debate over the power of monetary policy, the New Classical Economics also began to take hold. Many of the first generation started out as Keynesians, like Robert Lucas, Edward Prescott, Neil Wallace, and Thomas Sargent. And their explanations of why they became economists—interest in social problems such as the Great Depression—are strikingly similar to those of the Kennedy era Keynesians. But they produced a strikingly different theory.

New Classical Economics is not a criticism of Keynesianism, or a different mix of the same basic elements, but an entirely new way of looking at the economy. Unlike Keynesian theories, which are not overly difficult to explain to the uninitiated, a formal expression of the NCE involves capturing the dynamic aspects of the economy through a lot of impenetrable math. Essentially, however, the NCE stands on the following legs:

NCE takes the pivotal assumption in microeconomics—that markets work—and applies it to macroeconomics. On the face of it, this may not seem to be a major achievement. Nonetheless, the chief theoretical embarrassment for Keynesian economists is that their assumption that markets work in the micro realm doesn't translate into their macro framework, where they assume that market failures abound. For example, a key tenet of microeconomics is that prices adjust so that buyers and sellers can make transactions. That is, if prices are too high for buyers, sellers will lower them. (That doesn't mean the adjustment happens instantly; it might, in the case of wages specified in a labor contract, take some time.) In the macro world, however, Keynesians assume that markets do not adjust—they "fail" in the sense that prices do not fall in recognition of diminished demand by buyers. NCE assumes that markets adjust, period.

NCE also translates the micro notion of maximization, or optimization, into the macro realm. Maximization means that when given a choice, people choose what they prefer. Microeconomics assumes that people maximize by furthering their own best interests. By assuming that the same holds true in the macro realm, NCE argues that people react to changes in the economy either by taking advantage of opportunities created or by protecting themselves from adverse events.

The third leg of NCE is the assumption of rational expectations. People very quickly form expectations about the future that are accurate and are, as well, rapidly updated as new information becomes available. That is, we all anticipate the future rather like chess players who think not only of their next move, but their opponents' probable response and their counterresponse. People will not continue to make the same mistakes; they will not systemically underestimate inflation, for example. Moreover, since people learn from their mistakes and have the same access to information that the government has, they can anticipate government's response to that information and act defensively or offensively. And if one assumes that people in the economy optimize, then one must also assume that the economy is optimizing.

Thus, contrary to the Friedman hypothesis above, expectations about inflation will not lag actual inflation and correctly anticipated monetary policy will not even have a temporary impact on employment or output. (Rational expectations does not mean that people are endowed with perfect foresight or that their information is perfect. People will still make mistakes, just different mistakes, and they will use whatever information is available to them in making decisions.)

New Classical Economics shows why it is difficult for the government to surprise people into behaving against their best interests. Moreover, it demonstrates that by anticipating government action, people can render that action ineffective. Simply put, the New Classical Economics offers a theoretical explanation for the failure of activist government to deliver on its promise of managing the economy.

Consider what happens when alarm over the size of the budget deficit grows. People anticipate that the government will try to reduce the deficit by raising taxes. Since we act in our own best interest, we will protect ourselves from the coming tax hike (and the resulting fall in our aftertax income) by saving more money. But when we save more, we spend less, which, in turn, slows the economy and depresses tax revenues. The result is that policy will be checkmated: The government will end up with less revenue, not more; and of course the budget deficit may grow larger.

Same goes for devices such as investment tax credits to boost private investment. If businesspeople suspect that the government will offer investment inducements to pump up the economy when economic growth slows, they will then hold back on such investments waiting for the inducement. The result is to slow the economy even more.

Ditto for the practice of hyping the economy with inflation and then jawboning labor into keeping its wage demands below the ensuing rate of inflation. Workers will not accept inflation-reduced wages year after year. They will demand that labor contracts reflect the rate of inflation with cost-of-living adjustments, and this indexing in turn will defeat the two-step policy of both creating inflation and controlling it with wage-and-price guide-posts.

In other words, New Classical Economic models of economic behavior fly in the face of the Keynesian notion that government can alter policies and predict the outcome because people's re-sponses are not affected by the changes. In reality, people change their strategies when the government changes its strategies. In-deed, most NCE economists would argue that government inter-vention in the market only causes confusion and second-guessing and can be downright dangerous.

It is, by the way, this dynamic element that makes the NCE models so fancy. They must reflect the fact that the economic envi-ronment is an ongoing game played by several forces. When one force moves, the others will counter to further their interests. The models themselves, which critics complain are excessively difficult mathematically, come from physics and engineering models that search for the best solution over time. As one such adept, Paul Romer at the University of California-Berkeley, explains, "If one wants to, for example, engineer a rocket trip to the moon, one is solving a problem that involves a sequence over time; what the rocket does now influences what the rocket will do next."

At any rate, all this yields a very different view of business cy-cles (or, more properly put, uneven growth rates in real output) and economic policy than the old Keynesian model. In that model, failure of the growth rate to maintain itself was the result of market imperfections, and government activity was used to try to smooth the cycle and sustain growth rates.

New Classical Economics offers two ways of accounting for uneven growth. One view holds that since people have limited in-formation and often must guess at things, misperceptions and mistakes are inevitable—even when decisions are rational. Unpredictable movements in the money supply, for example, muddy the conditions under which workers and businesspeople make decisions. If businesspeople see that prices for their products are going up, they have to decide whether it's because their product is suddenly in demand or the general price level has gone up. If they guess wrong—say, they think demand for their product is increasing—they will make the wrong decision. In this case, businesspeople might invest in more machinery to make more products, producing an "up" in the cycle. Of course, the firms that guessed wrong will then find themselves sitting with a lot of unsold inventory and investment will fall, producing a "down" in the cycle. This doesn't mean that businesspeople were irrational, only that their information was imperfect and they made a mistake.

Another view of fluctuations, called real business cycle theory—the "real" means that the impact of monetary policy is not accounted for—hinges on the supply and demand "shocks" that are continuously bombarding the economy. These shocks can be bad, like strikes or war, or they can be good, like technological advances or excellent weather. If the economy is hit by a string of bad shocks of large magnitude, then a recession ensues. If, on the other hand, the economy experiences a string of good shocks, then a boom occurs.

Many shocks are the result of forces well beyond the control of the government. Some, however, are caused by government— from OPEC's oil shocks, to burdensome taxes or regulations, to just plain stop-and-go policies that make long-range planning impossible. In other words, the government is just one of many players or forces acting on the economy. Its actions—bad or good—can be swamped by other forces like droughts, epidemics, scientific breakthroughs, etc.

Most real business cycle theorists argue that the ups and downs of the economy are a natural consequence of the optimal responses of people to shocks coming from outside the economy. That is, the economy—all of us—responds to both good and bad events as best it can, causing fluctuations in activity. But these ups and down aren't a sign that something is deeply wrong; rather, since we are all responding the best we can, any government attempt to remedy the shocks is bound to make some of us worse off.

Both views argue for a more passive approach to policy and are backed by growing empirical evidence that government cannot offset normal fluctuations in output or employment or, worse, that the results of most interventionist policies are uncertain or may even be negative. Thus, NCE comes down on the side of stable policies. The government should specify its rules—monetary and fiscal policies—so people know what their opportunities and the probable consequences of their decisions are. Rules should not undergo frequent changes.

There have been two heavy-duty criticisms of NCE. First, that it promotes the view that government activism is just plain ineffective and should not be attempted at all, and, second, that its assumptions live in the twilight zone.

It is certainly true that NCE has cast doubt on some of our most cherished notions about government power to fix or manage things. Just the argument that expectations are rational strips monetary policy of much of its ability to affect unemployment or output. And it is surely true that all NCE arguments tend toward the conclusion that the government should refrain from short-term meddling in the economy. Since the economy responds optimally to shocks, then policy changes have a limited chance of making things "better," and even if such policies worked, they are undesirable because they generate uncertainty and inefficient second-guessing.

At any rate, arguing that government can't manage the economy, and shouldn't, is not the same as arguing that policy is irrelevant. Many New Classical economists are very interested in the impact of government policy, particularly in its role of promoting or hindering growth. Robert Lucas of the University of Chicago, for example, emphasizes the importance of human capital, suggesting that since a lot of business learning takes place under the stimulation of trade, trade should be as free as possible.

Paul Romer's ideas focus on the importance of technological change. He argues that since the development of knowledge and innovation depend on firms' being able to capture monopoly profits, factors like patent law—which confer a monopoly—are key. Robert King, at the University of Rochester, agrees, pointing out that even something like laws governing patent disclosure—the United States has relatively loose ones—mean that firms may delay filing for patents for fear their discoveries will be copycatted.

A second criticism is that NCE is driven by unrealistic assumptions. Perhaps the most nettlesome ones are that markets work and if everybody in the economy is optimizing, then the economy is optimizing; or as one real business cycle theorist puts it, "Irrational models require people to know too little, rational ones require people to know too much."

This is a cheap shot. Most models, no matter what school of thought, involve extreme and simple assumptions. Furthermore, the assumption that people are rational is surely more reasonable than the reverse. As for the idea that markets work, that is clearly more credible than believing, for instance, that there are big profit opportunities that go unrecognized over time.

Perhaps as frustrating to the uninitiated—particularly journalists used to talking about the impact of every tiny government action and tracing each wiggle of weekly figures to some story or another—is NCE's refusal to take any wiggles seriously. Most NCE-heads talk about their theories with amazing diffidence. "It all depends . . ." is the answer to most questions that begin with "What will be the impact of . . . ?"

A classic example is Robert Lucas's response to my question in 1992 of whether he was optimistic about the economy: "This country is going to grow at 3 percent a year no matter what happens. One administration, like the current one, can mess things up, but that's all transient. There's an incredible amount of stability in the last 100 years of U.S. economic history. I don't know why it's there and, of course, it could disappear at any moment."

Not that when the NCE does dabble in predictions, do their models yield better results than other models. In July 1982, Thomas Sargent was asked by interviewers about the Reagan administration's policies of coupling a very tight monetary stance with a very loose fiscal approach embodied in cutting taxes. A big mistake, he said: "It's not only not going to bring inflation down; it'll probably make it worse eventually. . . . If you were committed to Reagan's objectives and that's a big if, which are roughly to decrease the size of government and try to stimulate private investment, you try to leave taxes unaltered—and undertake measures to reduce the size of government and run a very loose monetary policy. Supposing he did get his tax cut and has these big deficits, his second-best policy is still to run a low interest rate policy, even if you have big deficits. You'd have high inflation but you're probably going to have that anyway because of the big deficits."

Of course, Reagan's approach, which did swell the deficit, did not result in big inflation but, rather, disinflation.

Ten years later, I asked Lucas about that prediction. "Sargent and I were talking as if it was going to be a year or two down the road; that's way off. Our method of forecasting future government spending and revenues was way off. Sargent and I imagined these deficits going on forever growing and observed correctly enough that that's impossible. Well, with a simple extrapolation of the current deficit it's pretty bad forecasting. . . . Of course, the Cold War ended too and we just lucked out."

Forecasting errors aside, the New Classical Economics swept the 1970s. By the end of the decade, its impact on academic economics was profound. It was even heralded in an April 1980 *Time* magazine cover story, which said: "The economics profession, which for four decades was dominated by John Maynard Keynes' disciples, who stressed a strong stimulative role for the government in the economy, is now swinging away from state solutions."

Of course, having a profound impact on academic economics is not the same as having influence in Washington and other places where policy is plied. And here NCE hasn't been very successful. Some of the blame belongs to the New Classical economists themselves, who eschew the traditional means of influence, like writing op-eds, testifying before Congress, or even—heaven forbid—joining an administration. Some of that is the same sort of arrogance and snobbery displayed by the early Keynesians—we are better, you are benighted. Some of it is due to the sheer hopelessness at changing a giant government apparatus dedicated to perpetuating itself through policy. But, to be fair, some of the problem is also due to a reluctance to go public before the models are "perfect"; and some because it is very hard to get one's point across with pages and pages of mathematical models.

There was, however, one bitsy, surprising ray of light recently. A chapter in the 1990 *Economic Report of the President* came very close to stating the new classical credo for policy makers. It was called, harmlessly, "Design of Fiscal, Monetary, and Financial Policies," but its content was dyn-o-mite. For the first time in the long history of the *Economic Report,* the Council economists present a coherent and well-developed analysis of the process and impact of policy making.

The arguments are very similar to what the New Classical economists had been preaching for over a decade. The Council granted that controversies exist among Keynesians, monetarists, supply-siders, and New Classical economists, but comes down on the general agreement that shortsighted policy maneuvers are damaging to the economy and that there are "great advantages in making a credible commitment to a policy plan."

The economists distinguish two approaches to policy making—discretionary and systematic. Discretionary means reacting to every little wiggle in the economy and systematic means a stated commitment to a clear rule of behavior; for example, tax rates will remain at x percent no matter what, or the federal budget deficit will be reduced by x amount every year come hell or high water.

The case against discretionary policy is threefold, according to the Council. First, since most businesses and consumers are forward-looking, expectations of future tax rates, inflation, and government programs affect their decisions. Frequent and unanticipated changes involved in discretionary policy making thus cause uncertainty for the private sector and make long-term planning difficult.

Second, if the government doesn't commit itself to a clear plan, there is always the temptation to change policies to achieve short-term gain that results in inconsistent policies. Such policy changes can have detrimental long-term effects. For example, an injection of fiscal stimulus by increasing government spending can lead to excessive spending, or a loose monetary policy could promote inflation.

And, finally, discretionary policy doesn't always work. Using policy to move the economy in the right direction at the right time depends on too many difficult steps: making a correct forecast, choosing the right policy, and suffering the inevitable lag between action and effect.

The economists then illustrated their argument in favor of systematic policies with an example of how inflation, monetary policy, and expectations interact by spinning out several scenarios.

Say workers are not expecting inflation. They do not demand increases to compensate for the erosion of their real earnings by inflation. Business's costs of production will not rise so rapidly and increases in their product prices can be relatively low. Thus, an unexpected monetary expansion will produce a pickup in demand that will stimulate firms to expand employment. Under these circumstances, a moderate increase in inflation may, in fact, lead temporarily to lower unemployment.

But in a second scenario, say workers eventually notice the pickup in inflation. The expectation of inflation will be reflected in their wage demands and firms will incorporate it into their price increases; this eliminates the fall in real wages and results in a return of the unemployment rate to its initial level. Because it's impossible to fool people indefinitely about the rate of inflation, higher inflation cannot permanently lower the unemployment rate. Moreover, higher inflation may not reduce unemployment at all. Take the case in which inflation persists. People aren't stupid, so they will begin to anticipate inflation. To the extent that people correctly expect inflation, even the temporary boom from a monetary expansion would be thwarted.

Simply put, in most possible scenarios, high and variable rates of inflation don't add anything to the party. On the other hand, if inflation is low and predictable, it will have little adverse effect on the economy. So what's the appropriate policy to achieve that? First, policy must be systematic—it must clearly specify a plan for, or a rule governing, the growth rate of the money supply; and, second, it must be credible—if people expect it to be implemented, they will act on that expectation.

Suppose the Fed announced that it was going to lower the

rate of inflation over a specific period and, to achieve this goal, slowed the growth of the money supply and allowed interest rates to rise. If the policy was not viewed as credible—for example, if people thought the Fed would weaken when interest rates got "too high"—workers and firms would continue to set wages and prices in expectation of inflation. Meanwhile, tight money would dampen demand and production. Thus the lack of policy credibility would result in a worsening of the economy as inflation remained high and unemployment rose.

Suppose, on the other hand, that the public believed the Fed would stick to its guns. Then the more restrained monetary policy would be accompanied by a drop in inflationary expectations. Tight money would have a smaller effect on unemployment and production, the period of slack would be shorter, and output would return to its potential but with less inflation than before.

The economists don't mean to suggest, however, that all policy, just because it is systematic and credible, is good policy. In some circumstances—for example, by reducing barriers to saving—fiscal policy can improve economic performance. But if policy is poorly designed—such as a tax system with high marginal rates—it will reduce incentives for productive activity and result in lower growth.

In some ways, this chapter from the 1990 *Economic Report* serves to highlight the trouble New Classical Economics has had and is having in being accepted as an alternative to activist government. After getting all that good advice from his economists, President Bush went right on trying to adjust economic policy to every little economic and political turn of events. Indeed, it's a huge understatement to point out that there has been, since the 1980s, a great schism between the New Classical Economics espoused by an academic elite and the activist economics practiced by policy honchos.

Too bad. As the next part demonstrates, NCE comes very close to explaining the uneven rates of economic growth since the 1960s and why an activist government had such little positive impact.

Part V

What
Really Happened
from 1960 to 1995

11

Good Circumstances, Bad Policy: The 1960s

B etween 1961 and 1968, the economy grew powerfully and convincingly at a real, average annual rate of 4.6 percent (3.8 percent for the entire decade) and per capita growth trended strongly upward. In the first half of the decade, there was also reasonable price stability and falling unemployment.

But just why all that nifty stuff happened isn't entirely clear. At the time, it was claimed by the Keynesians that the omnipotent, wise force known as economic policy was managing the economy and doing a damn fine job. Not only would it have been an act of self-abnegation for Keynesians to reject the credit, but it seemed more than reasonable to accept it. They were, after all, directing economic events from Washington.

Or were they? A broader look at the economy reveals that something much less simple and exact was going on, and that the belief that economic policy had a lot to do with it was based on a lucky coincidence between the debut of Keynesian theory and seven years of economic good times. Indeed, a broader look, which places economic policy in its proper context, reveals that the strength of global forces was powerful enough to overcome policy mistakes and miscues.

To begin with, the 1960s were part of the incredible two-decade burst of unusually strong worldwide growth that began in 1950. Between 1948 and 1971, world industrial production achieved new highs in average annual rates of growth. In fact, although U.S. growth was good, it was not as good as Western Europe or Japan (where the "catching-up" process after World War II played a big role). During the 1960s, real per capita income in most of the developed countries rose 50 percent—a record jump for a single decade.

What, then, was going on in the world beyond the United States? What accounts for the widespread burst of great times?

Much of this good fortune can be credited to an explosion in trade. Explosion isn't hyperbole, either. After 1945, the rate of growth in world trade exceeded the rate of growth in world output. This trade growth brought massive benefits to global consumers in the form of cheaper and better goods. More to the point, during the 1950s and 1960s, the U.S. economy was uniquely positioned to benefit from all this trade, especially on the export side, because it had emerged from World War II as the only nondevastated industrial economy.

The explosion in trade was possible because the trading nations were determined to overcome obstacles that had been erected before World War II. To that end, they created a new institution—the General Agreement on Tariffs and Trade in 1946—to reduce trade barriers. Negotiations among the industrial nations began in 1947. Shortly thereafter, 23 countries signed the first GATT accord; it consisted of over 100 separate agreements that covered half of world trade.

The success of the first GATT then provided steady momentum toward freer trade. By the mid-1950s, average tariffs had fallen from over 40 percent to under 25 percent and the GATT covered 34 countries, accounting for more than 80 percent of world trade. By the end of the 1960s, average tariffs had dropped to just over 10 percent. Part of the zoom in world trade came also from the flow of ideas as U.S. companies transformed themselves into multinational corporations, taking their production methods and managerial organizations with them.

Cheap energy was another fortunate factor for both the world and the United States. During the postwar period, there was tremendous growth in energy consumption. Total world consumption tripled—ditto for the United States—fueled by the needs of industry, cars, and home appliances. (This was, after all, the era of the great, finned gas guzzler.) Yet despite this surge in demand, the real price of oil fell 50 percent between 1950 and 1970. This piece of large luck was due to both abundant U.S. supplies and discoveries of oil in the Middle East.

And, finally, there was a burst of technological advancement. Because of the economic interruptions of the Great Depression and World War II, much of the technology created in the 1930s and 1940s was not fully exploited until the 1950s and 1960s. In the 1930s, for example, the rocket, helicopter, diesel train, electron microscope, radar, television and tape recorder, plexiglass and nylon were invented; in the 1940s came the transistor, DDT, penicillin and streptomycin—and the ballpoint pen. World War II also gave a great boost; most of the country's science and technology were mobilized to work on war projects that led, in turn, to advances in electronics and medicine. This avalanche generated high growth rates in productivity in the 1950s and 1960s—between 1960 and 1969, productivity increased at an annual rate of almost 3 percent.

There was also a spectacular burst in research and development. Some of that was due to government spending on defense, aerospace, nuclear energy, and space research and development. In the mid-1960s, a decline in the space budget was balanced by increases in research and development for health, energy, and agriculture.

But there was also a boom in private research and development—private spending peaked as share of the economy in 1969 (and didn't rebound to those levels until 1979). About 75 percent of private research and development was focused on electronics, chemicals, machinery and transportation. High-technology sectors had the greatest growth, followed by science-related, research-intensive industries like pharmaceuticals, petrochemicals, and precision instruments. This abundance of invention and innovation also fueled international economic growth as other countries caught up to the United States. In *The Machine That Changed the World,* for instance, the authors describe how mass production of autos didn't really take hold in Europe until the 1950s—30 years after Henry Ford had pioneered high-volume techniques in the United States.

All told, the great growth in the United States during the 1960s was generated partly by forces outside its boundaries and chiefly outside the management of economic policy. Of purely domestic impetuses, there were probably only two—the boom created by the war in Vietnam and the lowering of corporate tax rates in 1964, only one of which can be attributed to enlightened economic policy.

But if the good fortune wasn't due to Keynesian economic management, does that let Keynesianism off the hook for the bad stuff? And there was bad stuff, which, by the end of the 1960s, was beginning to attract attention as the problems with activist policy began to become apparent. Even to Keynesians.

The biggest disillusionment with the New Economics was its failure to remedy—or even explain—growing inflation. In 1961, the rate of inflation was barely 1 percent; by 1968, inflation was over 4 percent. Not for a moment did Keynesians think that loose monetary policy by the Federal Reserve was culpable; not for a moment did they think that the key to keeping inflation in check was to keep the growth of the money supply in check. Too bad; it is entirely possible that if money growth had been kept to the real rate of growth of the economy, the 1960s would have been inflation-free. Instead, loose fiscal policy—in the form of the budget deficit—was financed through inflationary means, with the Federal Reserve motoring out more and more money. Once the growth rate of the money supply increased from its low point in the 1960 recession, it kept accelerating—from 4 percent to 5 percent to over 8 percent a year. By 1967, people just expected inflation to continue.

Other flaws in Keynesian economics proceeded directly from its centerpiece notion about government activism. To begin with, government action was not the split-second, turn-on-a-dime kind that Keynesians envisioned. Rather, it could be glacial. This was called the lag problem. It became apparent that there were several lags associated with policy decisions. First, some time passed before a problem was recognized, and then additional time passed before it was understood to be persistent and thus in need of action. Second, it took time to develop a policy response. Then, of course, it took more time to get the policy accepted and operating. And, finally, once the policy was in effect, more time passed before its impact was felt.

Simply put, the length of time before the problem was sighted, understood, and the policy response operational could mean that prescriptions were coming on line too late to do any good but just in time to create mischief. It also became apparent that government action based on economic forecasting was dicey—the tools for predicting the course of the economy did not yield dependable, accurate results.

A related difficulty was that government's thrashing about in the policy climate—even if lag problems were controllable—unsettled the economic weather. This was, for example, the experience with the investment tax credit: tax breaks rained down one day, while the next day brought a tax drought; a week later, heavy rain again. An uncertain fiscal environment became one more stress for people to factor into their decisions.

This uncertainty eventually had two unintended effects, both of which worked to nullify the impact of active policy. In the case of tax changes, people learned to anticipate them—speeding up investment if it looked as though government would rescind the breaks or holding off on investment if it looked as though government would reinstate them. Or, as with the income tax surcharge in 1968, people ignored it and kept on spending, knowing that it was temporary.

Another problem with government activism could be sighted by the end of the 1960s—government was becoming a larger part of the economy. As discussed earlier, by the 1960s, speedy growth in the Soviet Union and the less developed countries made growth a fashionable issue. And Keynesian theory, by proclaiming that it could increase the rate of growth through government activism, became the rage. As things turned out, though, increased government spending discouraged private investment and thus perpetuated the problem it was trying to correct. That, in turn, called forth more government spending.

A great generator of government spending was, of course, the expansion of social programs. Beyond Social Security and Medicare, there were two policies that had a mega-impact on the federal budget—the poverty programs that began in 1964 (part of the emphasis on using government to redistribute income) and the environmental programs that started in 1961. (At first, poverty spending grew faster than environmental; indeed, programs such as the Air and Radon Act of 1961, the Solid Waste Disposal Act of 1965, and the Federal Motor Vehicle Emissions Act of 1967 cost just pennies compared with the environmental legislation that came later.)

Another malign result of Keynesianism, one barely evident at the end of the 1960s, was the use of budget deficits as a tool for stimulating the economy. (I say barely evident because the budget was briefly in surplus in 1966 and 1968, creating the false confidence that a deficit could be reduced to zero at a moment's notice.) So complete was the victory of deficit mongers by the end of the decade that almost no one even dared mention a notion that had been popular at the start of the decade—balancing the federal budget over the course of a business cycle.

In sum, the heritage of Keynesian policies was not pretty— loose money, fine tuning, increasing government domination of the economy and budget deficits. But perhaps the most destructive legacy of the 1960s was the sense that government policy could control events.

The conceit behind government activism was, after all, that the government could fix things. Reading the literature of the New Economics is like following a story in which economists, using their forecasting tools, espy threats to the economy. They then call upon "policy" to make things come right—no kidding, the phrase "policy was called upon" appears frequently in the economic reports of the president—and, in fact, between 1961 and 1969, policy was very busy; for example, it was called upon to make nine major changes in the tax laws and take on larger and larger public spending burdens. After a while, it's hard not to think of "policy" as a wise person with awesome powers.

Chief among policy's powers was, supposedly, the power to put an end to the business cycle, or economic fluctuations, so that growth could go forward continuously. No down periods. Thus every time the economy wobbled, policy was rushed into action to make an adjustment in fiscal or monetary affairs and correct the wobble. (Granted: One shouldn't make too much of presidents and policy makers declaring the end of the business cycle—that's politics. But, amusingly, and somewhat touchingly, optimism over the death of the business cycle found its way into official bureaucratic pronouncement, too. In November 1968, the Bureau of the Census's monthly publication of economic data known as *Business Cycle Development* changed its title to *Business Conditions Digest.*)

The fact that these mistaken notions did not derail the economy is testimony to the strength of the positive global forces that were propelling growth during the 1960s.

But the sneaker in all this is that when events beyond policy makers' control turned against them in the 1970s, people expected them to make things right. Having taken the credit for the good events in the 1960s, policy makers were called upon to do the impossible in the 1970s and, when they failed, to take the blame.

12

Bad Circumstances, Bad Policy: The 1970s

The decade of the 1970s was a dismal time for both the economy and policy makers—which makes it an excellent example of how forces beyond the reach of government can swamp the best and determined intentions of active policies. It also provides a neat demonstration of how activist policies can create their own bad climate.

There is no question that nine years of economic rule under Keynesian doctrines in the 1960s left the country with a bunch of problems—an overvalued dollar, inflation, increasing government interference in the economy, and a bankrupt economic theology. But the next decade also suffered from a dramatic and unhappy change in external circumstance. In short, the good luck of the 1960s turned sour. And just as the fortune of the 1960s was unusually good, the bad luck of the 1970s was unusually grim.

Chief among the unfortunate changes was that much of the

global good luck evaporated in the events that had driven economic growth: Advances in trade and innovation slowed, energy prices spiked up, and productivity growth lagged. This bad luck was not, of course, experienced by the United States alone. As all the industrial democracies enjoyed good times in the 1960s, so they all confronted various degrees of these problems in the 1970s.

Few enjoy sitting idle while things go wrong. But policy makers, both Democrats and Republicans, who had mistaken the good luck of the 1960s for wise management, generated their own set of bad circumstances as they responded to the limping economy. Their somewhat frantic efforts resulted in more government spending, more taxes, more regulation, and much more erratic fiscal and monetary policies. These, in turn, compounded the bad luck. The more government tried to manage the economy into better times, the worse the economy got.

Hence, the 1970s were a time in which inflation became entrenched, unemployment aggravated, the dollar weaker, and economic growth disappointing. The economy started the decade with no growth, experienced negative growth for two of its years, and began the first year of the 1980s by shrinking again; the average annual rate of real growth during the 1970s was less than 2.8 percent. Worse, real per capita income fell in three years during the decade. In all, the 1970s were brutal for policy makers. Those who still believed in an activist government emerged from this decade shaken and chastised.

An explanation of the events of the 1970s should start at the beginning of the spiral with three of the factors that had pushed economic growth during the 1960s to skyrocket pace—trade, innovation, and productivity. In the 1970s, all three turned mulish.

Although trade continued to increase during the decade, 1968 marked a deceleration in its growth rate, particularly for the United States; and, in 1975, the rate of growth slowed significantly again.

Thus, by the mid-1970s, while the volume of world trade continued to increase, it did so at a slower rate than world output.

Some of this slackening was due to the proliferation of non-tariff trade barriers, like Voluntary Restraint Agreements and countervailing duties. The Trade Act of 1974, for example, gave the president power to punish countries deemed "unfair traders" and granted several large industries protection from imports from developing countries.

Likewise, the burst of innovation in some science-based sectors fizzled. Some of the slowdown was due to broad cycles in science in which periods of discovery are followed by periods of quiescence; and some was due to a shift in focus—as economic conditions worsened, industrial research and development became less concerned with finding new products and more with improving existing ones. But some of the slowdown was also the result of increased government regulation. Pharmaceuticals and agricultural chemicals, for example, were especially hard hit by stricter safety and environmental standards.

The deteriorating economy also shrunk investment in new technology. Private expenditures on research and development peaked in 1969 and fell throughout the 1970s. The share of federal spending on research and development reached a peak of about two-thirds the total in the mid-1960s and declined substantially after that.

Productivity growth, too, languished, with the rate actually turning negative for several years. Although productivity is notoriously hard to measure, it's a safe observation that while the rate of growth in the 1960s achieved an annual average rate of 3 percent, it was almost flat in the 1970s.

Just why productivity slumped is still pretty much a mystery. There are many explanations, but no smoking gun. The best that can be done is to identify several events that coincided with the drop-off. Some of those events were due to bad policy, some were due to structural changes in the economy only indirectly affected by policy. Some can be attributed to specific and measurable causes; others to vague charges that business organizations had become inefficient or that the work ethic was fading. Most obviously, productivity growth was slowed by the double whammy of rising energy costs and antipollution regulations that not only increased production costs but also resulted in the widespread premature scrapping of equipment.

Changes in the labor force also had a negative impact. There was a shift from higher to lower productivity occupations as the mix of economic activity underwent structural changes, favoring less efficient industries. Smaller sectors like agriculture, fishing, forestry, and mining continued to shrink and become more efficient while lower-productivity sectors, like the service industry—finance, insurance, real estate, health, education, transportation, wholesale and retail trades, and public service—continued to grow.

Too, the quality of the workforce declined. Workers were increasingly less educated and more inexperienced—this last due to an influx of baby boomers and women. At the same time that its quality was declining, labor started getting more expensive. Beginning in the early 1970s, real compensation, which includes employer contributions to Social Security, pensions, and health insurance, rose sharply.

Finally, misplaced confidence in the government's talent to steer the economy also had an unfortunate effect on business practices. To the extent that business began to depend on government activism to keep demand for its products high and growing, bad management resulted. Price hikes, wage giveaways, and other lazy behavior that eventually made U.S. business—such as autos and steel—less productive and uncompetitive came, in part, from the expectation that government could keep the economy moving. Businesses grown fat and careless were also less able to compete internationally (and, of course, were the driving force behind the erection of trade barriers).

At any rate, the slowing of these growth rockets—trade, innovation, and productivity—played themselves out over the decade. While each factor was modest and fairly unremarkable by itself, taken all together, however, their impact was devastating. Particularly as they were accompanied by the more dramatic events of three price shocks.

The real price of oil, which had declined during the 1960s, soared during most of the 1970s. In October 1973, OPEC began cutting production and, one by one, its members embargoed oil to the United States. By the time the embargo ended in March 1974, the price of oil had quadrupled. (Although most of the impetus for the embargo was U.S. support for Israel during the Arab-Israeli war, OPEC was also concerned that the value of oil, which was priced in dollars, had been cheapened by the weak dollar and inflation.) In 1978–79, there was another oil shock. Taken together, these two shocks ran up the price of energy eightfold during the 1970s.

It is hard to overstate the impact of a sudden and large increase in the price of such a basic economic input as energy. After both oil shocks, business productivity dropped like a stone. Not only was the cost structure of much of the economy remarkably higher almost overnight, but the price run-ups meant a redistribution of hundreds of billions of dollars from oil-consuming countries, like the United States, to oil-producing countries. (In 1973, Western Europe and Japan took giant steps to reduce dependence on imported oil, so that by 1977, they were importing less oil in volume than before the shock. In the United States, however, oil imports continued to rise, further deteriorating the balance of payments and leaving the United States more vulnerable to the second oil shock.)

A third sudden and large price shock occurred in the early 1970s, when bad harvests, worldwide, compounded by low stockpiles of grain in the United States, ballooned food prices.

And, of course, all the above was aggravated by government policy. The 1970s suffered from one wrongheaded policy after another.

In retrospect, probably the most harmful was Nixon's 1971 decision to take the dollar—and the rest of the world—off the gold standard. The breakdown of the discipline of the gold standard allowed the United States to try to inflate its way through difficulties, thereby creating a lot of financial instability.

For instance, consider the immediate result of the demise of the gold standard. Fast money growth fueled more inflation, which spread from labor to raw materials and agriculture in 1972–73 and stiffened OPEC's resolve to raise the price of oil. At the same time, heavy selling of the dollar, which continued for the rest of the decade, pushed the dollar down, and down, and helped push inflation up. The end result was that by 1979, loose money had boosted the rate of inflation from a little over 5 percent a year to over 11 percent.

Escalating inflation also pushed up interest rates as rates moved higher to reflect an inflation premium. Despite these high interest rates, however, the combination of high inflation and the unindexed tax system made aftertax returns to savers negative for much of the late 1970s, thereby flattening the savings rate and further aggravating interest rates. One final note on inflation: While it looks as though the Standard & Poor's Index of 500 stocks rose, ending the decade slightly higher, the inflation-adjusted S&P 500 shows that stock prices actually fell almost 40 percent between 1969 and 1977.

Profligate monetary policy was not the only silly government activity during the 1970s. Fiscal policy was out of control as well. Federal spending increased substantially, from an annual average of 19 percent of the economy in 1961 to 20 percent in 1969 and to 23 percent from 1970 to 1979.

Just as significant was the change in its composition. Policy emphasis shifted from creating income to redistributing it. By the late 1970s, the federal government was spending more on transfer payments to individuals than on purchases of goods and services. For example, spending on Social Security and Medicare continued to zoom—while total benefits trebled during the 1960s, they more than quadrupled during the 1970s. Overall spending on social welfare peaked in 1976 at 60 percent of government spending and almost 20 percent of total economic activity. This redistribution of income was a great success, at least in terms of the data: there was a sharp reduction in poverty, from 22 percent of the population in the early 1960s to 12 percent by 1979.

Taxes in the 1970s went up, too, particularly in the last half of the decade, when tax revenue reached almost 20 percent of the economy. The largest increases came from bracket creep pushing people into higher marginal income tax rates. By mid-decade, high marginal rates were no longer a burden only on the rich: For every additional dollar earned by a middle-class family, almost one-half was eaten by taxes. The result was that the standard of living for most working, taxpaying Americans hardly improved—most of the gains in income came from increased employment (like the two-earner family) and not from productivity or real after-tax wage increases. At the same time, business was subject to higher effective marginal tax rates because the system failed to index for inflation, was based on historical depreciation rather than replacement costs, and taxed dividends twice.

Despite higher taxes, however, even higher levels of government spending enlarged the federal budget deficits. The deficit began the decade at a modest 0.5 percent of the economy, cratered to over 4 percent in 1976, but ended, in 1979, at 1.7 percent (and 2.8 percent in 1980). At no time during the decade was the budget balanced, let alone in surplus.

Misguided government policy also reduced productivity growth in several ways. First, rising levels of federal spending, taxes, and inflation discouraged private spending and investment. At the same time that private saving and investment rates were falling, the funds that were available flowed into less productive activities. Money was directed into residential housing at the expense of plant and equipment because of the combined effect of the preferential tax treatment for housing, increases in marginal tax rates, and inflation. And, lastly, the proliferation of government regulations hindered innovation, increased the cost of production, and lowered returns on capital.

Zealous regulatory policies were another factor that added to the economic woes, not only by pushing up costs, but by increasing uncertainty, and thus reducing investment and innovation. The Nixon administration probably imposed more new regulation on the economy than any administration since the New Deal. In addition to the biggie of wage and price controls, it also regulated, or controlled, energy prices and sharply extended federal regulation into the environment, occupational health and safety, and consumer product safety. This regulatory extension also caused compliance costs to soar—by 1979, such costs were running about $120 billion a year.

The only saving grace in this picture is that the major deregulation effort in transportation, telecommunications, and finance, which started slowly in the early 1970s, had picked up speed by the end of the decade. Although that began to reduce the cost of regulation by 1978, important gains weren't realized until the 1980s.

And, finally, quite apart from the fact that the policies themselves were damaging, was the destructive impact of all the uncertainty created by each administration as it flip-flopped. When the economy started to slow in the early 1970s, it was almost inexorable that policy makers began to apply the tenets of an activist government more feverishly. Consider the frantic efforts of the three administrations of the 1970s.

Richard Nixon ran as a conservative. He said he believed in the free market system. But his approach to governing showed him to be as interventionist as the next guy. Not to put too fine a point on it, but the Nixon administration policies show how embedded the Keynesian optimism about government activism had become. Fooling around with fiscal and monetary policy had become the thing to do. People expected it. Pundits demanded it. Politicians were more than happy to oblige.

This bias toward micromanagement placed Nixon a bit apart from his Council. As Republicans, the economists were not by and large Keynesian enthusiasts. Paul McCracken, Nixon's chief economist, had misgivings about government activism and the notion of fine tuning. Reinforcing this distance between the boss and his economists was Nixon's total lack of interest in economics. McCracken told interviewers later, "Mr. Nixon may have had an almost psychological block about economics."

The Nixon administration tried mightily to vanquish inflation and perk up growth. The result was that its economic policy was all over the place: from moderation (holding down federal spending and growth in the money supply) to absolutism (a wage-price freeze); absolutism was then relaxed (tight controls on wages and prices) and relaxed again (looser controls); relaxation gave way to another bout of absolutism (a wage-price freeze) and that, in turn, was followed by a policy of moderation (dismantling controls).

Nothing worked, and that left the next president, Gerald Ford, with a mess. In fact, his first year in office, 1974, was an awful year; it was the first full year to feel the impact of the quadrupling of oil prices, the run-up in food prices, and the first year of the stagflation that continued for the rest of the decade. Ford responded with an anti-inflation program. The problem was that just as it was announced, the recession worsened. By the end of the year, it was clear that the economy was in deep trouble; the Consumer Price Index was up 12 percent over the year before, unemployment was more than 7 percent, and economic activity had shrunk.

Consequently, in 1975, Ford shifted gears with a proposal to fight the recession; he called for temporary tax cuts, a rise in the investment tax credit, moderate budget restraint, and looser monetary policy. He also, crucially and disappointingly, abandoned fiscal conservatism in favor of deficit spending—producing what turned out to be the largest peacetime deficit to that date, to be exact, representing 3.5 percent of the economy. At any rate, just as Ford was pulling his about-face, the recession bottomed out (with unemployment reaching a postwar high of 9 percent) and by the third quarter of 1975, economic activity was growing at a 13.4 percent annual rate—the highest quarterly increase in 25 years.

One unusual attribute of the Ford administration should be mentioned. Despite the fact that he responded to pressures to "fix" the economy, his official rhetoric was very anti-activist, the result of both Ford's pro-business, antigovernment philosophy and that of his chief economist, Alan Greenspan.

Greenspan represented a clear break from the standard chairman of the Council of Economic Advisers. He had never been an academic economist; he did not have a Ph.D.; he ran a small business (economic forecasting); and he understood the financial markets and business. Moreover, Greenspan really was a believer in the free market, adamantly opposed, for example, to wage-price controls. By his own account, he came to Washington expecting the worst. "I was always ready to quit over policies I couldn't live with," Greenspan said years later. "I rented a furnished apartment at the Watergate and lived on a monthly lease for two and a half years." (When interviewed for this book, Greenspan was chairman of the Federal Reserve. Where did he live? At the Watergate; he owns his apartment.)

That the Ford administration's break with the business-as-usual of asking government to do everything was more in language than achievements matters only a little. It was the first time many ideas were seriously debated in official Washington: that there was no Phillips curve trade-off, federal spending was out of control, there was too much government regulation and interference in everyday life, monetary policy should be constant, there were costs—as well as benefits—attached to regulation, and that Social Security and Medicare spending were growing too fast. In all, it represented a significant departure from the language of the previous 13 years of Keynesianism.

During his 1976 presidential campaign, Jimmy Carter also took a strong anti-big-government stance (calling for a reduction in federal spending from 23 percent of the economy to 21 percent) and pledged to reduce the budget deficit (indeed, to balance the budget by 1981). But, once again, after the campaign was over, policy conservatism was swamped by the seductive promise of managing the economy and fine tuning became the plat du jour.

Charles Schultze, who was not heavily involved in the Carter campaign but became the chairman of the Council, recalls: "I figured that Carter's anti-big-government stuff was naive, that he wasn't serious." Schultze was right. The administration presided over three major policy shifts: The first aimed at stimulating the economy to quicken the recovery; that was replaced by an effort to fight inflation; that, in turn, was superseded by an attempt to overcome a recession. In fact, by 1981, the administration was unabashedly calling for higher spending and a bigger deficit—this, in the very year that Carter had promised to balance the budget.

Carter began his second presidential campaign burdened with responsibility for both inflation and an impending recession. He lost to Ronald Reagan. His back-and-forth policies had produced higher inflation, large budget deficits, slowing growth, and no improvement in unemployment.

On balance, these three administrations clearly represent the damaging side of the delusion that government can fine-tune or even direct the economy. When economic activity slowed, the impulse to have government do something became stronger, and the more government rushed to the rescue, the more it deepened the problems. Policy perspectives shrank to the very short term.

The dismal results of all this bad luck and bad policy are easy to read in a number we haven't looked at yet. During the 1960s, the unemployment rate averaged a little over 5 percent; during the 1970s, it averaged almost 7 percent—with a high of 8.5 percent in 1975. In fact, what happened during the 1970s has an official name—stagflation—a sickening combination of high inflation, high unemployment, and low growth. The dispiriting bottom line was that real per capita income fell in three out of nine years during the 1970s.

By the time the decade staggered to a close, it was not a pretty picture. People were worried. A *Time* cover story in August 1979 carried the headline: "To Set the Economy Right: The Rising Rebel Cry for Less Government; More Incentives and Investment." The article blamed the mess on too much federal spending, too rapid an expansion of the money supply, too much expensive government regulation. And who made this mess? "Economists, proud and powerful in the 1960s, now look like Napoleon's generals decamping from Moscow. Their past prescriptions—tax tinkering and Government spending to prop up demand, wage and price guidelines to hold down inflation—have been as helpful as snake oil."

Harsh words from a former cheerleader of the Keynesian effort. And there was more. In an April 1980 cover story, *Time* accused runaway regulation of undermining the basic freedom and incentives that allow capitalism to work: "When public budgets became tighter in the early 1970s, officials saw Government regulation as the means of achieving their social goals. Rather than spending billions of tax dollars to clean up the air and water, authorities passed laws obliging companies to spend large sums to do the job."

Time goes on to say: "Managers see themselves as Prometheus bound, unable to launch a new product or finance research into a tempting field without completing a fat book of federal forms and paying exorbitant, sometimes needless expenses." A businessperson tells the magazine that it is difficult to consider investments in projects because "we do not know what the Government regulations will be for pricing, importing, entitlements allocations."

In retrospect, economic policy during the 1970s has the aspect of both a Keystone Kops chase scene and Lucille Ball being inundated on the assembly line by tiny candy balls. It's low comedy to think of the federal government pushing and pulling, slapping and cajoling, the economy from one day to the next. But it wasn't at all amusing while it was being lived. People were thrown out of work, life savings were decimated by inflation, firms went out of business under price controls, low productivity eroded the standard of living, and all the while there was a feeling that events were totally out of control. It was clear that activist policies had totally failed by the end of the decade, and the rush to blame was understandable.

Understandable. But a touch misplaced. Blame was due also to bad luck in global events. Or bad timing. Certainly, as the 1960s saw a bunching of favorable circumstances, the 1970s experienced a clump of unfavorable ones. But the delusion that policy was wise and powerful had made it an easy target. A 1980 *Time* story quoted the head of the Organization for Economic Co-operation and Development: "It is quite clear now that in the industrialized democracies we let the success of the 1960s go to our heads. In responding to rising economic and social aspirations of our people, we have become overloaded, overregulated and insufficiently profitable."

13

Okay Circumstances, Okay Policy: The 1980s

The decade of the 1980s was a lot kinder to the economy than the 1970s; a lot kinder. That proved rather a relief since the decade looked anything but promising in its first year. The recession in progress was nasty: Growth was negative, interest rates were screechingly high, and inflation was out of control. It's fair to say that the economy was in relatively more trouble than any time since the Great Depression. Yet, over the decade, real economic growth averaged well over 2.5 percent, inflation came down swiftly, and, importantly, per capita income, which fell in 1982, grew strongly during the rest of the decade.

But, still, the 1980s weren't as good as the 1960s. Many economists, like Allan Meltzer of Carnegie-Mellon, explain the difference globally, saying, "Growth in the 1980s was part of a worldwide return to normal growth versus the supernormal growth in the 1960s and the subnormal record of the 1970s." And he is right. But why the return to normal? Just as a number of external factors made the 1960s so hot and their absence, combined with some novel negatives like the oil shocks, made the 1970s so blah, the 1980s both benefitted and suffered from broader forces.

Probably the most negative factor was slow trade growth: Increases in world trade lagged world output. Exports and imports continued to increase, of course, but so did the number and value of stuff subject to special protection or trade barriers. Protectionist sentiments, which started to be heard in the late 1960s, intensified during the 1970s and continued to grow louder during the 1980s. Both exporters and importers had complaints: In the first half of the decade, a strong dollar hurt exporters, and during the last part of the decade, a weak dollar hurt importers. But the main impetus for protection came from growing and effective foreign competition in industries in which the United States had once enjoyed a virtual monopoly lock: autos, steel, consumer electronics, machine tools, and textiles.

As a result, a bunch of high-profile industries sought and received shelter: autos, steel, sugar, textiles, and semiconductors. They were joined by hundreds of smaller industries, such as prepared mushrooms, heavy motorcycles, water beds, and roses. While not all these industries succeeded in protecting their markets, those that did cost the economy plenty in the form of higher prices and fewer choices. Estimates of how much each job "saved" cost per year in a protected industry varies from $40,000 (textiles) to $240,000 (autos) and total annual costs ran in the billions of dollars.

There were some positive trade events, of course. Free Trade Agreement talks with Canada, the United States' biggest trading partner, started in 1986 and were concluded successfully in 1988. And, in 1986, the Uruguay round of the GATT talks, involving some 108 nations, to eliminate tariffs and bring agriculture, intellectual property rights, and services under GATT were opened; in 1988 came the start toward a U.S.-Mexican Free Trade Agreement. But the economic value of these advances wasn't felt until this decade.

A second dampening factor was slow growth in productivity. The droop in the rate of growth that began in the 1970s showed only a bit of improvement in the 1980s. Again, nobody really can explain productivity—or be sure it is measured accurately. Many factors, for example, were offered to explain its fall in the 1970s: rising energy costs, antipollution regulations, changes in the workforce, structural changes in economic activity away from high-productivity sectors to low ones, big swings in fiscal and monetary policy, rising federal spending, skewed tax laws, and the proliferation of government regulations. The lackluster performance of productivity in the 1980s can be explained by many of these same factors, along with a new one—the dampening effect that changes in the interpretation of tort law had on innovation.

Tort law is the civil law covering harm that results from negligent actions of others, like injuries from defective products or medical malpractice; it is supposed to deter such negligence by compensating the injured. One of the rules governing accident law is strict liability, which focuses on whether the product that caused injury was defective in a way that made it unreasonably dangerous. Here is where the problem arose.

In the 1960s, the courts began to expand the rule of strict liability. The argument was that the liability rule would give producers an incentive to prevent accidents; moreover, producers could easily provide insurance for unpreventable injuries by charging higher product prices. This approach resulted in no-fault liability. Unsurprisingly, by the mid-1970s, product-liability cases were surging.

The trouble is that no-fault liability increases defendants' tort costs and, with it, their need for insurance coverage. Thus, as the years rolled on, costs associated with liability insurance skyrock-eted. Bad enough. But, worse, sometimes producers preferred to take a product off the market because insurance was too pricey or even unavailable. Potential liability costs, of course, also have a chilling effect on investment in innovation. Simply put, stiff product-liability rules became part of the constellation of factors hindering advances in productivity.

These two deleterious forces were countered by several more benign developments. For one, there were advances in technology during the 1980s. Ceramics—inorganic, nonmetallic materials that can operate under very high temperatures—and fiber optics—glasslike strips that can carry lots of information efficiently and ac-curately—were developed and applied. Likewise, the machine tool industry became adept at using microprocessors and laser scan-ners. And, too, the pharmaceutical industry brought many impor-tant discoveries to market in the 1980s. There may even be innovations whose importance won't be known for decades. But, generally, innovation in the 1980s was made up of lots of little steps, the kind of progress that doesn't make, at least at first, for big leaps in growth.

Another positive force was the decline in the price of energy. Real oil prices, which had reached an all-time high of almost $31 a barrel in the early 1980s, declined sharply after 1985, to $13.75 a barrel. Energy was relatively cheap for the last part of the decade.

And, finally, policy contributed to a good climate for growth. The crucial factor was that no large mistakes were made—or at least not many—and a few beneficial policies were followed.

Most important, Reagan stood firm behind the Fed in its fight against inflationary monetary policy. The result was that inflation was reduced more rapidly than anticipated: It fell from 1980 through 1983 and remained pretty much stable around 4 percent until the end of the decade.

Tax policy, too, was a plus. Although there were a lot of changes during the 1980s, it moved in a mostly consistent and positive direction. Marginal income tax rates were reduced substantially: the top rate came down from 70 percent to less than 34 percent, rates for median-income taxpayers were reduced by over 30 percent, and millions of low-income people no longer paid any income tax.

However, some of the reduction in tax rates was financed by shifting taxes to the future, via the deficit, or by increasing taxes on new investments. There were also increases in Social Security taxes mandated in 1983, which, by the end of the decade, had mitigated other tax reductions. After falling briefly to levels almost as low as 1960, tax revenue as a share of the economy was 18 to 19 percent in 1989, the same as it had been in 1979. But, on balance, the structure of the tax system was more growth-oriented.

After that, however, the policy record gets weaker. Spending as a share of the economy went up, smartly, before beginning to fall. Overall, the Reagan administration did succeed in reducing the pace of government spending from what it was under the Carter administration, but, of course, all things are relative, and spending still represented well over one-fifth of economic activity.

But the composition of government spending changed—count that as a positive. From the late 1960s to 1980, government's primary goal had shifted from increasing to redistributing income and wealth. The category with the largest growth was transfer payments to individuals (Social Security, Medicare, education, and so forth). In 1960, transfer payments absorbed about one-quarter of the budget and by 1981, they accounted for one-half. Most of the increase was generated by the expansion of entitlement programs—particularly Social Security—where, as eligibility expanded, so did benefits. For example, in 1980 dollars, the average benefit paid to a retired worker was $191 a month in 1960 and

$341 in 1980. Further, as the share devoted to transfer payments rose, the share going to defense fell, so that spending for defense fell from 11 percent of the economy in 1962 to 6 percent in 1980.

The 1980s reversed some of that direction. Spending for social welfare was fairly stable during the 1980s, down from the high (as a share of both the economy and government spending) in the mid-1970s; and spending cuts were made in other domestic programs. Real defense spending accelerated—investments in equipment and a significant rise in military pay raised the defense share of the economy to almost 7 percent in 1986 before declining to under 6 percent.

As for regulation, the 1980s record was mixed. Spending on regulation fell by almost a billion dollars a year. There was also some further deregulation of the economy during the early 1980s; but mostly it followed the path set out in the Carter administration, with efforts to deregulate finance, telecommunications, and transportation. Prices fell, saving consumers hundreds of billions of dollars as these three industries experienced a burst of competition, increased innovation, and rising productivity. (These benefits continue, saving the economy at least $40 billion a year.)

But just at the moment when the benefits of deregulation became clear, Reagan allowed the momentum to slow. Worse, the administration did nothing to stop the march of social regulation. More than half a dozen laws regulating the environment were passed, costing over $100 billion a year. Safety regulations added another $30 billion a year. Indeed, during the 1980s, the direct and indirect costs of regulation came to almost $400 billion annually.

Too, the federal budget deficit was surely a blight. As a share of the economy, it reached its high point in 1983 at over 6 percent, although, by 1989, the deficit had sunk to its lowest level in seven years at 2.9 percent of the economy. It is difficult to assess the impact of the burgeoning deficit; it did not cause high interest rates or inflation—two of the most feared results. It did, on the other hand, decimate national savings and prompt higher taxes later on.

Trade policy, as already mentioned, was a loser. Despite its rhetoric favoring free trade, the administration imposed more new restraints on trade than any other administration in the postwar period—it was during Reagan's first term that the first Voluntary Restraint Agreement limiting imports of Japanese cars was negotiated, as were extensions of the Multifibre Agreement limiting textile imports and the Voluntary Restraint Agreement limiting steel imports.

Even the administration's trade successes were mixed. In 1983, for example, Congress and the administration agreed on an omnibus trade law that generally supported freer trade. The major provision of the Trade and Tariff Act of 1984 was the renewal, until 1993, of provisions eliminating tariffs on imports from developing countries. But less virtuous, the act did not cover some major imports, notably textiles. Moreover, the new act extended provisions that provided specific authority for the president to retaliate against barriers to U.S. exports, including unfair trade practices, and expanded the countervailing duty statutes.

Looked at more broadly, the Reagan administration did mark an abrupt change from the economic approach taken during the 1960s and 1970s. Instead of rushing around to respond to every real and predicted economic glitch, the administration tried to take a long and consistent view, treating government intervention as a hindrance and stressing private initiative and markets.

This change is evident in the language of the administration's economic reports of the president. Indeed, the 1982 *Report* shows the distance traveled since the Keynesians had authored the 1962 *Report*. Gone entirely is the 1960s view of the world in which citizens wait patiently for wise and powerful government policies to lead them to the promised land. Government policy still has power in the 1980s view, of course, but it comes from its ability to create incentives for people—either productive impulses or wasteful ones. The Keynesian emphasis on fiscal policy is gone, too, replaced by two equal levers—fiscal and monetary. Some familiar powerhouses of policy, like taxes, are still touted, but gone completely are Keynesian concepts such as the potential economic growth rate, the gap between that and the actual growth rate, and the Phillips curve trade-off between inflation and unemployment.

Perhaps the most startling departure from past policy making happened early on in 1982. When that year's *Economic Report* was written, the very mean recession in progress was hardly mentioned. While the Reagan administration acknowledged it, no countercyclical policies were put forward to deal with it. Rather, the assumption was that the recession would work itself out more quickly and satisfactorily if the correct long-term policies were followed.

In this, the administration was following public feeling. In February of 1982, as unemployment was reaching 9 percent, a *Time* magazine cover story proclaimed that the traditional panaceas of bringing down unemployment with public works projects and jobs had been discredited: "Even many Democrats are skeptical that old methods should be tried again." *Time* reminds readers that while Congress passes such legislation during a recession, by the time the money gets into the economy, the recovery has begun and the extra spending just fuels inflation.

As Martin Feldstein, chairman of the Council in 1982, says, "It was absolutely amazing. There was almost no talk about short-term solutions." Feldstein goes on to point out that this was also a politically correct stance. Reagan's approval ratings were very high, despite the fact that unemployment was up, because the rate of inflation was coming down and inflation was what scared people. (However, as the recession appeared to drag on, the administration did sign off on a "jobs" bill that increased gas taxes to fund spending on highways and urban transit. Congress also passed its own emergency jobs act early in 1983. Since the recession bottomed out in November 1982, this money was spent after the recovery had started—as usual.)

Another outstanding difference between 1962 and 1982: Reagan was a president who knew what he wanted from, with, and for economic policy. Feldstein says that the question most asked by his colleagues was "Did Reagan understand economics?" His reply is yes. "At meetings, he always listened to presentations and forecasts, to endless tables on the budget. My first meeting with the president was unnerving. I briefed him on Third World debt; he didn't take notes, he asked very few questions. Then he told me an anecdote about something or other and that was that. It left me wondering. But a day later, the subject came up in a cabinet meeting and the president summarized what he had heard perfectly. He had a remarkably good memory for oral presentation and could fit information into his own philosophy and make decisions on it."

Reagan was also, as William Niskanen, a member of his Council, points out, sufficiently certain of his convictions to know when he was fudging. Niskanen tells the following story: "Reagan created the President's Economic Policy Board made up of old-line Republicans—business guys and old friends. The board met regularly to advise the president. When they started to press Reagan on his deteriorating trade policy, Reagan repeated the political spin, but he was uncomfortable. So he stopped calling board meetings. He didn't want to hear criticism from his friends when he knew he was wrong."

Nonetheless, a closer look reveals that the administration's economic thinking was not the revolutionary break claimed (triumphantly) by Reaganites or (hysterically) by their enemies. Much of the anti-big-government rhetoric had started with the Ford administration and continued, albeit soft-pedaled, with Carter. And, more to the point, although action began to match words with the Reagan administration in some things—less regulation and less taxes—other things, like government spending, were the same old story. For example, the administration promised to bring down both federal spending and the budget deficit (to under 20 percent and less than 2 percent of the economy, respectively), but federal spending and the budget deficit swelled.

In Reagan's first *Economic Report* letter, his sternest words concerned government activism. Reagan put the major share of the blame for poor economic growth in the 1970s on "ever greater intrusion of the government" and declared the path to better growth is through limiting the many roles of the federal government: less spending and taxing as a share of the economy; a smaller budget deficit; a reduction in regulation; and an eschewal of stop-and-go economic policies that, with their short-term focus, only exacerbated long-run problems.

The Council's section of the 1982 *Report* expanded these themes, emphasizing that its fiscal policy had two aspects. Fiscal policy itself—spending, taxes, and deficits—was cast in terms of its impact on people's decisions, "since it is these decisions that ultimately generate employment and growth." And, second, fiscal policies must be geared to the long term: "Households and business look to the future in making current economic decisions. The government has some direct influence on factor inputs, but its main influence is through the indirect and long-term incentives it provides to work and save."

The administration vowed to stick to its guns to avoid generating the uncertainty that comes from frequent changes and forecasted success only if its policies were credible in the eyes of the public. Only then would people work harder and save more in response to lower taxes on work and investment. Too, the administration argued that as soon as people realized that it was committed to maintaining its policies over the long haul, they would respond by lowering their expectations about inflation. And as those expectations came down, so would inflation.

And, finally, the administration argued that changes in spending made in an attempt to offset fluctuations in the economy had costs. Such changes, which increased the uncertainty faced by consumers and firms in making decisions, discouraged the supply of productive factors to the economy. Furthermore, these attempts may just make a bad situation worse.

All this wisdom seemed to be amply rewarded. By 1984, economic recovery was forcefully under way: Real growth had skyrocketed at a 6 percent pace in 1983, unemployment was falling, inflation was calm, and investment was healthy. As *Time* magazine put it in a cover story in March: "In many ways, the President of the U.S. could not ask for a better election year economy. . . . After presiding over a deep recession, Ronald Reagan can now boast of having engineered one of the most stunning economic turnarounds in decades."

By 1985, economic events had been going its way long enough for the Reagan economists to write an obituary for Keynesian economics. In its *Economic Report,* the Council recalled how, in the postwar period, economists had been optimistic that fiscal policy could be used to smooth out the business cycle. Subsequent experience, of course, was that policy often was formulated based on erroneous forecasts and was usually too late to help but right in time to hurt. But even if those glitches could be ironed out, economists were beginning to doubt whether fiscal policy had the economic impact it had been credited with.

The economists argued that activist fiscal policy was upsetting to private decision making. Too, since responses to changes in fiscal policy were often unpredictable, this uncertainty complicated both business and consumer planning. And, thus, the economists concluded, short-term policy changes should be avoided. Fiscal policy should be stable and predictable. And when there is a recession? Ditto. In fact, if policy makers didn't react, thereby creating even larger disturbances in the economy, the recession itself would be short and mild.

(Very sensible advice. But also very amusing coming from an administration that was busy making tax changes every year; in the next year came the Tax Reform Act of 1986, another major change in the structure of corporate and personal taxes.)

The last word of the Reagan administration was said in the *Economic Report* of 1989. It was about as smug and self-confident as one would expect from an administration that had presided over seven years of economic growth. Reagan blandly acknowledged one of the steepest recessions in the postwar period by calling it "a shaky start." He pointed out that the economy had expanded, in real terms, by an average of more than 4 percent a year (a tiny exaggeration). Reagan also offered a signature line: "We have at last learned that more government is not the solution to our problems; often it IS the problem."

And the administration did have some strong bragging points. Most significantly, since the expansion began in November 1982, the economy had grown almost 23 percent and buoyed living standards—as measured by real gross national product per capita—at an average annual rate of 3.2 percent.

Finally, was there a Reagan revolution? Not really. In terms of direction, Reagan did almost everything he promised, but certainly not to the extent he implied. In terms of government's role in the economy since 1960, it is fairer to say that the administration engineered either a mini-revolution or a mega-change. In terms of what's happened since the Reagan administration, however, it's fair to call the Reagan years an astonishing outburst of good sense.

Thus, one huge plus that was present in the 1980s—and notably absent during the 1960s and surely the 1970s—was the idea of limited and predictable government. For eight years, people could make decisions in a philosophically stable climate—in Reagan, they had a president whose views were known, strongly held, and unchanging. That kind of dependability removed a lot of uncertainty and second-guessing from the planning processes of business and households. No question there were policy changes, but most of the big ones were in the same direction. People didn't go to bed at night anxious that misplaced government zeal to respond to every problem, perceived or otherwise, would just create new ones in the morning.

In all, sensible policies did partly account for growth during the 1980s. On the fiscal side, for example, cutting marginal tax rates and fruits of deregulation fostered an attractive investment climate; on the monetary side, a stable, credible policy resulted in low inflation.

Charles Plosser, an economist at the University of Rochester, has a nice backhand way of summing it up: "The 1970s had mostly 'worse' shocks—oil, inflation, and protectionist trade policy—therefore instability was very high. The 1980s had fewer 'worse' shocks, fewer worldwide disturbances, and thus a more stable environment. So there was more stability and, in the absence of external shocks, a return to a normal growth path."

Simply put, perhaps the big lesson of the 1980s is that, absent large negative shocks coming from outside of the economy, growth can proceed at a congenial pace under mixed good-and-bad policy conditions—as long as the overall climate is somewhat stable and predictable.

14

Okay Circumstances, Bad Policy: The 1990s So Far

I t's dicey to say anything about the economic climate of a decade that's only half over, particularly because an assessment involves broad or global forces that only become apparent over a longer period. But, even at midpoint, one thing is clear. Many factors associated with good economic growth were in place during the early part of the decade: world trade was growing faster than world output, energy prices were mostly low, falling steadily from 1990 through 1994, the rate of productivity growth was perking up with average annual gains of around 2 percent, and inflation was relatively low and unthreatening. Yet, the economy did not preform up to expectations.

The decade began with a recession; although it lasted from mid-1990 to March 1991, making it three months shorter than the postwar average, the recovery was protracted, with subnormal growth in its first two years. Indeed, in the first half of the 1990s, economic growth logged a disappointing annual average of 2 percent, with real per capita income falling in one of those years

There are two obvious reasons for this dismal record: both bad external shocks and bad policy were able to overwhelm the favorable circumstances.

No question, the economy suffered just plain bad luck in the unusually horrible weather at the beginning of the decade. In 1989, came Hurricane Hugo in South Carolina, the Loma Prieta earthquake in northern California, and exceptionally cold weather. Three years later, the awful weather got more awful. Hurricane Andrew—the most destructive U.S. hurricane ever—came and what was called, probably rightly, the "storm of the century" hit the East Coast in 1993. The next year saw record snows in the Northeast and record warmth in the West. Then there were devastating floods in the Midwest, fires and an earthquake in California, and the Southeast and East were battered by 16 separate snow and ice storms.

Adding up lost days of work, lost sales, and physical damages, the cost was probably in the tens of billions of dollars. Nobody knows for sure, but bad weather could account for as much as 2 percent in lost growth. (Even though economic activity rebounds from natural disasters with faster growth due to spending for repairs, the economy is always and ultimately worse off because of the destruction.)

There was also a spot of trouble in the Persian Gulf in August 1990, when Iraq invaded and occupied Kuwait and threatened Saudi Arabia. Oil prices rose substantially on the world market; by the end of the year, futures' prices had spiked up to $40 a barrel. Nonetheless, the spike was short-lived and oil returned to its more normal price of around $20 by 1991, somewhat before the war ended, and continued to fall from there. Count energy prices as a brief negative.

And then there was bad economic policy—quite bad. The Bush administration was a grab bag of confusion, multiplying regulation, higher taxes, and increased government spending. The Clinton administration is not faring much better; after an initial burst of activism that, among other things, raised taxes and hammered the health care industry, it then subsided into policy drift—one policy today, another policy tomorrow.

Conventional wisdom lumps the Reagan and Bush administrations together as the Reagan-Bush years (or, more editorially, as the decade of greed). In one sense, the conventional wisdom is blameless: Bush's tenure as president began at the end of the 1980s, he was Reagan's vice president and he often identified himself with Reagan's approach, speaking about the need for long-term goals and minimalist government. But from the standpoint of economic policy, Bush belongs to the 1990s; his administration, which was jam-packed with ambitious plans for government activism, marked an abrupt departure from Reagan's policies. And although Bush was not able to advance much of his agenda, his policies came to fruition in the 1990s.

Even a cursory reading of his economic reports shows that Bush's critics were wrong; he did have an economic policy. In fact, he had many economic policies. And that was the problem; his goals seesawed abruptly from long-term growth to short-term stimulus, from regulating everything in sight to regulating nothing, from no new taxes to all kinds of taxes, and from lots of new government spending to no new spending.

The Council was headed by Stanford University professor Michael Boskin. While many are dismissive of Bush's grasp of economics, saying that the exercise frustrated him, Boskin says, "He was very literate about economics; he had strong ideas, but they were not as entrenched as Reagan's." The middle ground seems to be the observation that while Bush liked to think things through, he had no economic principles to guide him from one issue to another.

When Bush became president in 1989, the economic signals were mixed, with slowing growth and accelerating inflation. He proceeded to make things worse. Negotiations on what was to be the Budget Agreement of 1990 began and, by the summer, two important policy disciplines had fallen by the wayside—the read-my-lips-no-new-taxes pledge and the Gramm-Rudman law for reducing the federal budget deficit.

These major changes unsettled the economic climate. Equally worrisome was the debate over amendments to the Clean Air Act that confronted businesses, both large and small, with the possibility of having to spend tens of billions of dollars a year to control emissions. (A minor but real threat to business costs was also present in a bill to accommodate disabled Americans, which was also being debated.)

The final budget bill was set by late fall. Its goal was to cut the deficit by $500 billion over five years by increasing personal taxes, excise taxes, and user fees; it allowed for a substantial increase in federal spending while putting binding caps on discretionary spending. It also killed Gramm-Rudman, allowing deficit targets to be "adjusted" for changes in economic conditions. (It was also the occasion of the 10 percent luxury tax—that mother of poorly designed policies.) The Amendments to the Clean Air Act and the Americans with Disabilities Act were also passed by the end of the year.

No surprise that with all this uncertainty and increased actual costs (oil) and potential costs (clean air) overhanging the economy, growth slowed in the second quarter and turned negative in the third and fourth quarters of 1990. The recession had started.

Of course, no administration is going to take the blame for a slowdown, and the Bush administration did not, instead citing in its *Economic Report* something called "structural imbalances." Among these imbalances was weakness in the financial sector—the collapse in real estate, large amounts of debt held by consumers, corporations, and government, and the difficulty of small and medium-size business in getting bank credit.

Sure, but some of these weaknesses were also generated by policy mistakes. For example, an attempt to end the bad effects from partial deregulation of the banking system resulted in the Federal Deposit Insurance Corporation Improvement Act, passed late in 1991; the law didn't deal effectively with the perverse incentives created by deposit insurance, so it didn't improve anything. Indeed, the combination of that Act and the 1989 Financial Institutions Reform, Recovery and Enforcement Act may well have made things worse by tightening bank supervisory standards and capital requirements, thereby exacerbating the decline in real estate values and causing a credit shortage for business. In fact, the only policy mistake mentioned in that year's *Economic Report* was attributed to state and local governments that had raised taxes, thus dampening spending and "further impeding economic recovery." Funny—no mention was made of the federal government having just done the same thing.

As for its solutions to end the recession, the administration trumpeted some short-term fixes; for example, an acceleration of federal spending aimed at creating jobs and the return of income tax withholding so that about $25 billion could be spent immediately. Bush also announced a new, recession-fighting agenda: some proposals aimed at reducing taxes, which, remember, he had just raised; others were to revive real estate by allowing a $5,000 tax credit for first-time home buyers, penalty-free withdrawals from individual retirement accounts for first-time home buyers, and a tax deduction for losses on the sale of a personal residence. There were also plans for more government spending—record levels for

Head Start, research and development, infrastructure, math and science, anticrime and drug abuse, job training, and the creation of Enterprise Zones.

Stanford University professor John Taylor, then a member of the Council, agrees that many of the agenda items, like the housing subsidies and early release of withholding taxes, were very short-term. But, he says, "the demands to do something were really huge; on the political side, we had to show that we were doing something."

The economy in 1991 was a tad better than 1990. But not much. Growth, which had been sharply negative at the beginning of the year, flattened out on the slight positive side by year's end. Even though the recession had officially ended in March 1991, postrecession growth of 2.3 percent in 1992 was slow by historical standards; it was also the year in which Bush lost the presidential election.

The *Economic Report* for 1993, written after Bush lost to Clinton, was serious and astonishingly frank. Mistakes were admitted, self-congratulation was held to a minimum. David Bradford, a member of the Council explains: "The tone is more freewheeling because it was our last shot. We couldn't hurt the president then. The *Report* also didn't have as many reviews by the various agencies. Even the people at the agencies who did read it were leaving and not that interested."

The Council acknowledges without excuse the growth of government spending and faces up to the failure to reduce, or even control, the deficit, admitting that the Budget Agreement of 1990 was a flop because of its failure to get a grip on entitlement spending, most especially for Medicare and Medicaid.

Less straightforward, however, was the administration's answer to the fact that the longest peacetime expansion had come to an end on its watch. The economists begin on the highest possible plane, asking if carefully chosen policies can eliminate recessions entirely. "The answer, unfortunately, is that they almost certainly cannot." Why? Because two of the three types of events that may tip the economy into recession cannot be controlled.

The first type of event, called a structural adjustment, is something that may happen in response to policy—not a mistake but an important policy action. For example, a decision calling for a sharp reduction in defense spending will mean that production and employment will fall off while the economy reallocates resources. The second type of event is a shock that comes from outside the economy, such as OPEC's large and sudden oil price increases. And the third type of event, one that is controllable, is a policy mistake such as an unexpected broad tax increase. At any moment in time, the economy may be trying to overcome one or more adverse factors, so that when a bunch of bad events happen together, or a very large negative one hits the economy, a recession results.

Having all but rejected any activist policy remedy for a recession, the economists then descend into the nitty-gritty political question: Would different policies have helped shorten the recent recession? "The answer, in our opinion, is a qualified yes."

What they mean is that fiscal and monetary policy should have been more stimulative. This allows the administration to escape blame since it "proposed fiscal policies in early 1992 that would have provided a modest stimulus to the economy." The Council ends by saying that even perfect policies could not have prevented a recession, but if Bush's remedies had been tried, they may well have cushioned the downturn and sped the recovery.

Doubtful. The recession was both shallow and short precisely because the government—both the administration and Congress—was unable to enact the traditional "stimulus" to "manage" economic activity. The administration was lucky that its remedies were not tried because they consisted of just the things that belong in the category of damaging, short-term discretionary policy. Tax subsidies for first-time home buyers, for example, would have made matters worse in the long run by further distorting a tax system that directed too many resources into housing and too little for investment.

Those policies that did pass into law made things worse. Consider the inability to control spending. Money going to social programs like elementary education, child nutrition, Head Start, and Medicaid grew much faster than during the Reagan administration, achieving the same rate of growth as under Carter. Overall, domestic spending increased at almost twice the rate as it did under the Carter administration, bringing federal outlays to over 23 percent of the economy.

Accelerating spending meant that the Bush administration also failed to keep the deficit from rising (it had dropped to under 3 percent of the economy when Bush took office, but was back up to an almost 5 percent share by 1992). Nor did Bush keep taxes down, and he only belatedly tried to stop the explosion in regulation that he had initially permitted.

The only exception to these policy failures was trade, where the administration was fairly successful, ending its tenure with a major step toward the North American Free Trade Area among the United States, Canada, and Mexico—our first and third largest trading partners.

Then was the Bush administration responsible for the recession and slow recovery? It was certainly guiltless of several years of punishing weather and the buildup of structural imbalances that brought the long-anticipated end to a long upswing in the business cycle. But it must be declared guilty of policy mistakes: chiefly in new and costly regulations and the Budget Agreement of 1990. But perhaps the biggest failure was the administration's inability to keep its mouth shut. The answer to any question seemed to be another government policy, another initiative. It is no little irony that the Bush administration was succeeded by another administration that cannot keep its mouth shut either.

The Clinton administration came into office with a passionate belief in the power of government to make things better and insufficient attention to the power of government to make things worse. This failure in perception was aggravated by the fact that Clinton was a minority president; he received significantly less than half the popular vote (43 percent)—hardly a mandate for the many activist plans he put forward.

While the Bush administration took over an iffy situation, the Clinton administration inherited a very promising one—the economy was coming out of a recession, inflation was under 3 percent, interest rates were low, energy was cheap. And after many years of blabber, the NAFTA trade pact had been successfully concluded and looked legislatively achievable. Yet, the administration was unable to capitalize on these factors: economic growth during 1993, its first year in office, was barely 3 percent—well below the 5 to 6 percent rates traditionally associated with a recovery. Unemployment remained stubbornly high.

Why was the economy underperforming? Most of the blame can be laid to bad policy. The Clinton administration was essentially another Bush administration—there were tax hikes and a plan-a-minute to fiddle with the distribution of resources in the economy. There was also a unique factor—a distinct lack of credibility in foreign policy, which meant lack of confidence in the dollar. The dollar, which had rallied briefly in the late 1980s, kept falling against major currencies during the 1990s, breaking many postwar records against the yen and deutsche mark.

Most crucially, after focusing on the limp economy during the presidential campaign of 1992, the Clinton administration then spent its first months in office in a very public display of indecision about an economic program. Eventually, the administration de-cided to raise taxes—no tax cut for the middle class as had been solemnly promised during the campaign.

Along with the very public muddle over the administration's economic program came the very private deliberations over health care reform—that secrecy left one-seventh of the economy in the dark about its future. In short, the administration managed to stall the great engine of economic growth, consumer spending, by con-fusing and scaring people. Indeed, consumer confidence, which had shot up after November 1992, peaked in January 1993 and fell throughout the year, erasing all its gains.

The administration's faith in the abilities of government was evident in its first *Economic Report*. It praised a number of new ini-tiatives, including the National Service program, a new program of empowerment zones and enterprise communities, and several new technology programs; it noted increased funding for research into new environmental technologies, comprising nearly 50 initiatives to reduce U.S. greenhouse gas emissions, and promised to spend more on education and job training. Gone entirely are the lectures against fine tuning or the evils of regulation, or pleas for less gov-ernment; instead, the emphasis is on market failures and the power of government to do good.

The heart of the administration's activist philosophy was con-tained in a chapter called "Microeconomic Initiatives to Improve Efficiency and Productivity." The essay started with a little lesson on how markets work to provide us with what we want and need. After this nod to Adam Smith, however, the economists warned that there is a hitch: "Yet markets are not flawless. They may, for example, become controlled by monopolies, generate excessive pollution, or lead to insufficient investment in research and devel-opment. Through collective action, we can sometimes correct such market failures and thereby improve the ability of private markets to serve social goals." No surprise, administration economists claimed to have just the ticket for correcting these flaws in the market system. Then followed another list of initiatives: some were totally vague—"promoting efficiency in the public and private sectors, addressing environmental externalities and promoting technology"; some sounded like campaign slogans—reinventing government, regulation of natural monopolies like the information superhighway, and a plea for less greenhouse gas.

During the administration's second year in office, the economy was better—real growth picked up to a 4 percent annual rate—but it was still running at nowhere near recovery potential. This was especially disappointing since inflation remained low and steady at under 3 percent, unemployment fell, and, most importantly, the rate of growth in productivity logged a second year of solid increases. Once again, some blame lies with the administration's policies. Chief among them was, of course, the health care reform disaster.

After many months of clandestine meetings with secret participants, the administration unveiled a mammoth plan to reform the nation's health care system. Initially, the impetus was to control costs. The main idea was to insure the uninsured because the uninsured allowed medical problems to escalate until a crisis was reached and they appeared in emergency rooms, where they got very expensive care. The idea of controlling costs, however, was lost in the pages and pages of a complicated scheme to promote a "managed care" system covering everybody by assigning them to vast bureaucracies.

The public was confused, policy makers were sharply divided, most health care professionals were outraged, and the rest of the health care industry was hostile. After a yearlong battle, during which many alternative schemes were advanced by friends and foes, opinion polls showed that there was little support for any of the proposals and reform was dropped. But not in time to prevent damage—investment in biotechnology had dropped to almost zero and many docs were stampeded into joining HMOs.

Late in 1994, an angry and exhausted public spoke up. The November congressional elections, which turned the Democrats out of the House and the Senate, giving those two bodies a Republican majority, were widely interpreted as a vast repudiation of Clinton's tenure. Pollsters reported that voters were fed up with big government, big spending, big deficits, big taxes, big, period.

While this is a rather dramatic example of how an overactive government can gum up the works, that shouldn't take away from the basic point: Bad economic policy throughout the 1990s slowed growth from what it might have been, given rather good external events. Despite a decisive pickup in the rate of productivity growth, despite a significant surge in world trade (and the 1993 achievement of two major trade pacts, NAFTA and GATT), and despite low energy prices, the economy has limped along.

Conclusion: Now What?

No matter how one comes at the problem—up close and daily or broad and theoretical—the experience of the past 35 years demonstrates that government policy is not the powerhouse we thought. Why is it, then, that otherwise intelligent people still cleave to the idea?

Much of its force can be traced back to the 1960s, when the Keynesian economists came to Washington. Their mission was to convert the world to a new kind of partnership in which the government, through enlightened policy, gave life to their theories to provide the country with good, constant economic growth. These Keynesians were excellent preachers. And some of those ideas, which in retrospect seem totally harebrained, were accepted and put into practice. A wider acceptance of their ideas was due to a coincidence between the debut of government activism and unusually good economic growth in that decade. But the economy in the 1960s was good because of historical accident—positive global forces and fortunate external events. The fact that government activism didn't dilute those factors is proof of how powerful they were.

That Keynesian economics in practice didn't work is evident in its legacy—the problems that we are trying to solve today. That Keynesian economics could not ever work is obvious when its theoretical basis is examined.

Their key notion was that not all players on the field were equal. The most powerful was the government. Economic players in the private sector—all of us as consumers, investors, workers, or businesspeople—were thought to be passive recipients of policy. When the government instituted policies aimed at making us invest more, we would. When the government trotted out policies aimed at making us spend more, we would. It was a recipe book approach to economics: For every occasion, there was a dish; each dish had a recipe. Government policy makers would follow the recipe, diners would eat and be satisfied.

This theory also implied that the government was the most helpful agency for sorting things out and the most adept at getting things done. Thus, government was asked to take on an enormous responsibility for the economy—to respond to every bump with a policy solution that would keep growth strong and smooth.

At any rate, the idea took hold in the 1960s because it seemed to work. An activist government was pressed into service to speed up economic growth—and growth was good. So good and so persuasive, in fact, that the Republicans, who had dismissed the New Economics at first, were totally signed on by the time Nixon was elected.

But by then, the external climate that had actually generated the growth had soured. And even though the Nixon administration was a veritable frenzy of government activism and intrusion, nothing worked—the economy sagged. Indeed, the combination of the legacy of 1960s policies and those created by the frantic application of new policies aggravated tough times. The Ford administration realized this but, despite its stern rhetoric, was unable to resist the delusion that the economy could be managed. Ditto for the Carter administration.

And thus ended the dismal 1970s. The return to a more normal growth pattern in the 1980s was due to the return to both happier external factors and policies that exhibited less confidence in government's talents to do good and a deeper appreciation of government's ability to cause harm. By and large, the government was less active in trying to manage the economy. Policy was aimed at creating incentives, but with a broader understanding that the government cannot control human behavior, only create opportunities. When the Bush administration reversed this direction in the 1990s and started raising taxes and talking about short-term tinkering, it tipped a slowing economy into a recession.

The 1990s are, so far, a decade at war with itself. From a broad economic perspective, the U.S. economy should do at least as well as the 1980s—trade is growing smartly, productivity growth is up, energy prices seem well behaved. But, so far, this decade, having started with a return to the delusion of government activism in the Bush and Clinton administrations, is not living up to promise. Possibly the congressional elections in 1994, which demonstrated that voters are yearning for less government, will temper the hands of policy makers.

That SOMETHING should temper the hands of policy makers is clear. As New Classical Economics argues, and the past 35 years demonstrate, Keynesian theories are just plain wrong. For starters, the government is not more powerful—or more prescient—than other players. It is just one player among several, more powerful in some things, less powerful in others. For example, while government may follow the recipe correctly, diners think about whether they will have indigestion the next morning; that is, people have expectations about the consequences of policies. So their responses may not be what government anticipates, and policy making becomes a game of point, counterpoint, with people having the power to checkmate the government. That was what happened with the income tax surcharge in 1968; since it was temporary, people just ignored it and kept on spending, knowing it would be gone in the morning. And the economic boom, which the surcharge was supposed to stop, kept on booming.

Thus, what looks to policy makers like a simple exercise in incentives can be a complicated process of unintended consequences in reality—witness the luxury tax of 1990. The point is that consumers, investors, workers, and/or businesspeople are not stupid. If government asks them to do something they feel will undercut them, they won't do it. Consider the failure of the wage-price guideposts during inflation. Workers and firms will not willingly take wages or prices that do not compensate for the erosion of their purchasing power by inflation.

Another problem is that government policy may be swamped by external events. Technological innovation, for example, can be a powerful spur to fast growth and healthy increases in productivity. Certainly, this was true for the United States in the 1950s and 1960s. Not only can technological shocks be mightier than policy, they may even defeat it. Surely, the technological revolution in communications had a profound impact on the government's ability to implement policy. Just the capability to move vast sums of money around the world with a few keystrokes on a computer foiled attempts at "managing" the value of the dollar, or even maintaining the structure of the financial industry that was put in place in the 1940s.

The same goes for external events such as the weather. Bad weather and consequent bad harvests in the world in the early 1970s would have slowed growth in the affected countries regardless of how enlightened government policies were.

Nor is the government a more helpful agency than other players. When the economy is hit by a big, bad shock, private players respond based on their understanding of the consequences to them. When the government intrudes its own solution, it just creates more things for the private sector to have to take into account. For example, the oil shocks in the 1970s were damaging enough by zooming the price of energy; the government made the problem worse by "accommodating" the shocks through loose money, which made the resulting inflation impossible to control.

Moreover, the more the government engages in fine tuning to manage events, the less certain the economic environment becomes. Because people make decisions on the basis of their view of the future, the uncertainty created by a busy government tends to freeze decision making. That was clearly the case in the stock market crash of 1987 and, more recently, in early 1993, when Clinton announced all his major policy initiatives, especially health care reform, thereby smacking the wind out of both consumer confidence and the economic recovery.

Also, government busyness can generate a lot of inefficient second-guessing. Take the investment tax credit, which has been instituted, repealed, reinstituted, and rerepealed so many times that it fosters counterproductive incentives. If it is in a repealed state, then firms hold back from investing in slow times, expecting it to

245

be reinstated, thereby compounding the slow times. If it is in an enacted state, firms rush to invest before it is removed, thereby distorting growth.

Nor is the government more adept than private players; it does not operate with a better forecast of the future and is less flexible in responding to events. Part of this problem is, of course, the political process. Even if the government were terrifically and accurately farsighted, there are three branches of it, and each can have a say, putting its paw prints on the solution. That inevitably means that, at the end of the process, the solution is suboptimal in economic terms, although it may be optimal in political terms. This is surely true when government activism involves regulation— however meritorious the goal, government bureaucracies are not capable of managing and enforcing regulations without exacting an enormous cost to productivity.

Thus, although the idea of having a powerful, helpful, and adept government to take care of problems as they arise is a comforting one, it is a delusion. And it is a dangerous delusion, in part, because relying on the government to respond to every glitch unsettles the economic environment. It generates lots of inefficient second-guessing in the private sector about just what the government is going to do and how to respond, engenders unintended consequences, and creates regulatory gridlock.

And, finally, when activism is based on a flawed theory, as it was with Keynesianism, the damage to the economy can be severe in other ways. The results of the past 35 years are today's troubles evident in excessive regulation, unstable prices, a stubborn federal budget deficit, and a tax system that is unfair and cumbersome—all of which impede economic growth.

What should this mean for the future conduct of economic policy? Several things.

Conclusion: Now What?

First, we should realize that government has only a limited capacity to affect events or remedy bad breaks. If government tries to do too much, it steps on itself, hits consumers in the chest, trips up businesspeople, and unsettles investors.

Second, it follows that we should recognize just what it is that government can do, and ask only that. Government can create a friendly economic environment for the private sector to be innovative, produce, and employ people. A friendly environment is one that allows for plenty of opportunity for the private sector to fiddle around in without fear of the government gumming it up. That goes double for government regulation.

Such an environment would include big ticket items like low marginal tax rates, which strengthen incentives to work, save, and invest; less regulation, which frees up time and money for more productive uses; a sensible and steady monetary policy, which keeps inflation at low, predictable levels; less government spending, which keeps money in the private sector where it can be spent more efficiently; and free trade, which keeps U.S. business competitive and cost-effective and delivers lower prices and more choices to consumers. There are also smaller ticket items like speeding the process of innovation with stronger patent laws or loosening up immigration laws to make it easier for foreign scientists, engineers, or other high human capital immigrants to become U.S. citizens—or at least to work in this country. And reforming tort law—especially product liability—to restore incentives for innovation.

Third, we should ask the government to go about its business in a predictable, steady way. That means following policy rules, not engaging in discretionary or fine-tuning activities. By asking the government to focus on the long-term, there will be less thrashing about in the short-term. And with less thrashing about and more certainty, people will make fewer mistakes in responding to changes.

Fourth, we should have confidence in free markets. This is a rather schoolmarmish reminder, but the failure of communism has settled the debate over which is better—free markets or managed ones. This means restoring incentives to the private sector whenever possible; government should only undertake projects if it can produce a higher rate of return or demonstrates better judgment than the private sector.

Fifth, we should recognize that bad things happen. Sometimes, they happen randomly—flukes of fate—or sometimes because people make mistakes. The list of potential mistakes is a long one, ranging from making dopey investments to choosing an employer who goes bankrupt. They are lamentable. But we shouldn't ask the government to underwrite our mistakes. As Charles Plosser points out, when government starts subsidizing mistakes—or penalizing success, for that matter—it creates very perverse incentives.

The short and long of it is we should be ready to accept less government and more responsibility. Government should give us policies that are aimed at creating conditions for long-term growth and that are undertaken in a steady, predictable fashion. And we should be willing to explore opportunities, take risks, absorb failure, and stop running to the government to fix things that we think fall short of perfect.

The payoff should be a stronger economy. And that ain't peanuts. It's the only way to give people productive employment, deliver a better and better standard of living and a promising future for our children. The next decades will be tough for the economy. The aging of the population, for instance, will create greater demands on resources while generating fewer resources to call on—

particularly by increasing demands on the health care and retirement systems. The most effective way to guarantee that we aren't caught short is to start now to build the conditions for innovation, productivity, and growth.

ACKNOWLEDGMENTS

I tried to interview as many of the heads of the Council of Economic Advisers as I could. Sadly, some key figures, such as Walter Heller and Arthur Okun, are dead; in those cases (and for Gardner Ackley as well) I have relied on interviews in *The President and the Council of Economic Advisers: Interviews with CEA Chairmen,* edited by Erwin C. Hargrave and Samuel A. Morley (Boulder, Colo.: Westview Press, 1984). I also benefited from Arjo Klamer's *Conversations with Economists* (Totowa, N.J.: Rowman & Allanheld, 1984) and Nicolas Spulber's *Managing the American Economy, from Roosevelt to Reagan* (Bloomington: Indiana University Press, 1989).

I'm grateful to all the people who talked to me—especially those who suspected (correctly) that they would disagree with the result—including:

Martin Anderson, Kenneth Arrow, Alan Auerbach, Charles Bacall, Robert Bartley, Barbara Bergmann, Richard Bethea, Michael Boskin, David Bradford, Horace Busby, Joseph Coyne, John Donaldson, Patrick Dorsey, James Duesenberry, Victor Eubanks, Peggy Forbes, Martin Feldstein, Henry Fowler, James Gianforte, Alan Greenspan, Jim Gregory, Robert Hall, Linda Hooper, Hendrik Houthakker, Dale Jorgenson, Robert King, Marvin Kosters, Roy Levit, John Lewis, Sheldon London, Robert Lucas, Kathy Healy MacCrosland, Allan Meltzer, Joel Mokyr, Robert Mundell, Richard Nelson, Tom Nemet, William Niskanen, Charlie Palmer, Jack Pearson, Merton Peck, Charles Plosser, Edward Prescott, Paul Romer, Paul Samuelson, Charles Schultze, Gary Seevers, Leonard Silk, Barry Smith, Robert Solow, Jimmy Spradley, John Taylor, Jeff Tepper, James Tobin, Alexander Trowbridge, Linda Wilhelmy, and Ronald Winston.

I also want to thank the American Enterprise Institute in Washington, D.C., where I was the DeWitt Wallace–Reader's Digest Fellow in Communications in a Free Society during 1991–93. I am indebted to Evelyn Caldwell and Murray White; Irwin Stelzer and Chris Myers; and my able researchers: Heather Hogan, Carl Demeree, Maureen Griffin, and Timothy Kelly.

Also, lots of gratitude goes to those who read the manuscript in its various phases: Susan Chace, John Donaldson, Suzanne Garment, Nathan Greenlee, Sylvia Hiat, Colleen Kendall, Fran Kiernan, Dwight Lee, Jay Mann, Peter Martin, Aunt Blanche Mittleman, Peter Passell, Jon Previant, Russell Roberts, Lisa Schiffren, Leonard Silk, Barbara Smith, Gene Stone, Merryl Tisch, and Ken Weisshaar.

Many thanks are due as well to my agent, Ginger Barber; my editors, Bob Asahina and Sarah Pinckney; and Marianne Monesteri.

About the Author

Susan Lee has been deputy editor of *The New York Times'* op-ed page, a senior editor and columnist for *Forbes,* a columnist for *Vogue,* and a member of the editorial board of *The Wall Street Journal.* She received her Ph.D. in economic history from Columbia University, where she taught in the economics department. She is the author of *Susan Lee's ABZ's of Economics* and *Susan Lee's ABZ's of Money and Finance.* She lives in New York City.